GROWING UP
FATHERLESS

MIKE NAPPA

GROWING UP
FATHERLESS

Healing from the Absence of **Dad**

Fleming H. Revell

A Division of Baker Book House Co
Grand Rapids, Michigan 49516

Published by Fleming H. Revell
a division of Baker Book House Company
P.O. Box 6287, Grand Rapids, MI 49516-6287
www.bakerbooks.com

Second printing, July 2003

Printed in the United States of America

Library of Congress
Cataloging-in-Publication Data
Nappa, Mike, 1963–
   Growing up fatherless : healing from the absence of dad / Mike Nappa.
      p.   cm.
   Includes bibilographical references.
   ISBN 0-8007-5807-2 (pbk.)
   1. Spiritual life—Christianity. 2. God—Fatherhood. 3. Father and child—Religious aspects—Christianity. I. Title.
BV4509.5.N37 2003
231′.1—dc21   2002014647

Growing Up Fatherless is published in association with the literary agency, Nappaland Communications Inc. To contact a Nappaland author, access the free webzine for families at www.Nappaland.com.

For Anne, Janette, and Mary

A father to the fatherless, a defender of widows, is God in his holy dwelling. God sets the lonely in families . . .

Psalm 68:5–6

CONTENTS

INTRODUCTION

Just the Facts

Half of all children [in the U.S.] will witness the breakup of a parent's marriage. Of these, close to half will also see the breakup of a parent's second marriage."[1]

From 1979 to the present, more than two million adults *each year* have obtained a divorce in America.[2]

Christians are more likely than non-Christians to experience divorce. (Among Christians, 27 percent report they've gone through a divorce; only 24 percent of non-Christians report that they have.)[3]

Among people attending mainline Protestant churches, one in four (25 percent) has gone through a divorce; 29 percent of Baptists have gone through a divorce; and roughly one out of every three (34 percent) nondenominational Protestant church members have gone through a divorce.[4]

By the time they turn eighteen, more than half of American children have spent a "significant part of their childhood living apart from their fathers."[5]

The United States of America has the highest divorce rate in all the world.[6]

Divorce in America is a twenty-eight-billion-dollar-a-year industry.[7]

The generation of Americans with the highest divorce rate (37 percent) is Builders (people who were between the ages of fifty-three and seventy-two in the year 2000). Their children (Baby Boomers and first-wave GenXers) have experienced the greatest parental marriage disruption in all of American history.[8]

From 1970 to 1994, the number of divorced adults quadrupled, making "divorced persons" the fastest-growing marital status category in the United States.[9]

Forty percent of Generation X adults grew up as children of divorced parents.[10]

With 27 percent reporting a divorce, whites are more likely to get divorced than African Americans (22 percent), Hispanics (20 percent), or Asians (8 percent).[11]

Between 1950 and 1980, the number of children involved in divorces and annulments rose 175 percent.[12]

Since 1972 multiple millions of children *each year* have lived through the divorce of their parents.[13]

From 1970 to 1996, the number of children living in single-parent families more than doubled, from 12 percent (roughly one in eight children) to 28 percent (more than one in four).[14]

Among the millions of children who have seen their parents divorce, one of every ten will live through three or more parental marriage breakups.[15]

Studies in the early 1980s showed that children in repeat divorces earned lower grades in school, and their peers rated them as less pleasant to be around.[16]

Between 1970 and 1975, the divorce rate rocketed upward by 40 percent.[17]

Sixty percent of black women who married in the 1960s and early 1970s had already experienced a divorce by 1992.[18]

Forty percent of children growing up in America today are being raised without their father.[19]

The number of single fathers in America has tripled since 1980.[20]

Teenagers in single-parent families and in blended families (stepfamilies) are three times more likely to need psychological help within any given year.[21]

"Compared to children from homes disrupted by death, children from divorced homes have more psychological problems."[22]

Children living with both biological parents are 20 to 35 percent more physically healthy than children from broken homes.[23]

"Most victims of child molestation come from single-parent households or are the children of drug ring members."[24]

"A child living in a female-headed home is ten times more likely to be beaten or murdered."[25]

A study of children six years after a parental marriage breakup revealed that—even after all that time—these children tended to be "lonely, unhappy, anxious, and insecure."[26]

Children of divorce are four times more likely to report problems with peers and friends than are children whose parents have kept their marriages intact.[27]

Children of divorce, particularly boys, tend to be more aggressive toward others than those children whose parents did not divorce.[28]

A baby born to a college-educated single mother is more likely to die than is a baby born to a married high school dropout.[29]

Children of divorce are at a greater risk to experience injury, asthma, headaches, and speech defects than children whose parents have remained married.[30]

People who come from broken homes are almost twice as likely to attempt suicide than those who do not come from broken homes.[31]

Children of divorce are two to three times more likely to grow up with a parent who struggles with alcoholism than children from an intact marriage.[32]

Children of divorced parents are roughly two times more likely to drop out of high school than their peers who benefit from living with parents who did not divorce.[33]

Girls from a broken family are twice as likely to become teen mothers than girls living with biological parents who have not divorced.[34]

Seventy percent of long-term prison inmates grew up in broken homes.[35]

1

A Father Who Is There for You

My mother was cursing with great regularity into the telephone. To her credit, swearing was a habit she kept trying to quit, feeling it was inconsistent with her Christian faith. However, the man on the other end had so angered her that profanity spewed from her mouth like water from a spigot.

The man she was cursing was my father.

I sat in the other room, pretending not to listen but eavesdropping anyway. I was nine years old and the proud middle linebacker of my elementary school's football team. It was my first year playing ball. We had had an undefeated season and won the city championship. Pretty heady times for this little fourth grader!

To celebrate, my coaches had planned a father/son picnic and awards ceremony. We were all to bring our dads to this shindig where we would eat, laugh, play games, and receive our trophies. Or at least that's how it was supposed to be. What my coaches didn't know was that my dad hardly ever did anything with me. My parents had divorced when I was three, and after that a father was only a rare reality in my life. Still, he lived only about forty-five minutes away from me, so I decided to call and ask him to come.

When I got him on the phone, he chuckled, congratulated me on winning the championship, then said no, he wouldn't be going to the awards ceremony. No, he didn't have other plans. He just wasn't going to go.

When I hung up, my face must have displayed my disappointment, because minutes later Mom had Dad on the phone, cursing a royal blue streak into his ear. "You will go to that ceremony with your son," she ordered (with a few colorful bits of name-calling tucked in). "You will not disappoint Mikey by making him be the only boy on his team without a father there!" They argued a bit longer, and in the end, my father relented.

My stomach knotted up with both relief and apprehension. He was coming, but I knew he wouldn't want to be there. I felt like a piece of used bubble gum. But at least he was coming.

When the day arrived for the glorious event, my father dutifully picked me up on time and drove me to the park where the ceremony was to be held. That was when I discovered someone could be physically present yet altogether absent otherwise. Soon after we arrived, we split up. He stood for a moment with the other fathers, then went off by himself, virtually ignoring what was going on.

The coach was so proud of all of us boys that he called us up to the front, one by one, and regaled the rest of the dads with stories of how each of us contributed to the season. My coach remembered many details about each boy's play. My dad, on the other hand, had no memories of my championship season. He hadn't been there.

When it came my turn, the coach had the fathers laughing about how I wanted to play so bad, I tried to play without a helmet, about how I had contributed beyond my size and won the starting middle linebacker spot midway through the season. I looked for my dad in the crowd, hoping he was proud of what the coach was saying about his son. But he was back at the food table getting a bite to eat, not in the crowd with the other fathers.

After the ceremony, the next planned event was a friendly dads-against-sons football game. Some dads volunteered to play, others to referee, others to stand on the sidelines cheering.

My dad said it was time to go. I told him the program was only half over, but he'd put in his hour and he was ready to leave.

He dropped me off at home, then, just like always, he was gone.

Where's My Daddy?

Now, to be fair, you should know that my father wasn't a deadbeat dad. He always paid child support on time, always sent me a birthday card, and tried to live according to his Christian faith the best way he knew how. But when it came to being my father, he just wasn't there.

To be honest, I didn't miss him most days. But every so often I'd hit a lonely spot and desperately wish I had a father to talk to, a dad who would simply care about me enough to invest his life in mine. But I didn't have one, so I tried to be strong, until one late night when I was talking with my mom. Awkwardly, I was trying to figure out why other kids had dads, and I didn't. Finally, my mother said words that have stuck with me the rest of my life.

"Mikey," she said, "you may not have an earthly father, but you do have a heavenly Father. And he's always there, no matter what."

I didn't fully understand what that meant until years later when, as a sixteen-year-old, I became a Christian myself. But after that, whenever I felt the hole that divorce had put in my life, I remembered my mother's words and threw myself deep into the arms of God. I found he was always there.

When I graduated from high school, my father wasn't there, but my Father was.

When I went across the country to attend college, my father didn't drop me off at school and make sure I was all settled in before he left. But my Father was with me the whole time.

On my wedding day, my father stayed at home. But my Father stood with me at the altar and viewed the beauty that would be my wife coming down the aisle.

When I graduated from college, my father was nowhere to be found. But my Father cheered and smiled as I walked across the stage to receive my diploma.

When my son was born, my father didn't come to rejoice with me. But in the maternity ward at the hospital, my Father wrapped his arms around my son and me, welcoming my child into the world.

I could go on, but I think you get the point. After all, you've probably experienced some of the same things yourself. You know what it's like to long for a dad or a mom and have that longing go unfulfilled. You've felt the loneliness of adjusting to life without a parent, or the stress of trying to add a stepparent into your life to fill the gap. Those statistics you read in the introduction to this book aren't simply numbers to you, because you—like me—lived what those numbers represent.

But do you know that no matter what may have happened to the parents in your life, you've got one full-time, never-going-to-leave, always-available-to-talk, love-you-in-spite-of-yourself Father? It's true, whether you believe it or not. You've got a dad who will always be there, no matter what.

When I was a child, I knew that I wanted a parent. Now that I'm a man, I realize that I *need* a parent, and I believe you do too. I know, I know. We're past the hard part. Our childhoods in single-parent families or blended families are over, and hey, we survived—even excelled in some ways. What do we need parents for now?

Although we may be grown up on the outside, inside there remains the child we once were, the boy or girl who, once upon a time, wished for a mommy or daddy to make life better, longed for Mom or Dad to be around, to experience the joys and sorrows of our life.

That desire to be important in the eyes of a parent doesn't go away, no matter how old we get. We may suppress it, try to forget about it, even ignore or deny it. But deep down we know—I know, you know—we need a parent, even as adults.

The good news is I have One who will always be there for me, always make himself available when I call, always go with me when I want my Daddy nearby. I have God as my Father.

And you can have him too.

Your Father Is Always There

Listen to how King David described his relationship with his heavenly Father:

> Where can I go from your Spirit?
>   Where can I flee from your presence?
> If I go up to the heavens, you are there;
>   if I make my bed in the depths, you are there.
> If I rise on the wings of the dawn,
>   if I settle on the far side of the sea,
> even there your hand will guide me,
>   your right hand will hold me fast.
>
> Psalm 139:7–10

Now let me offer my own paraphrase of David's eloquent psalm:

Where can you and I go from our heavenly Father's
    presence?
If we get stuck in traffic on the freeway,
He is there.
If we find ourselves alone in our homes,
He is there.
If we wonder where he was when our parents divorced,
Wonder why he let that happen,
We can still look back and say he was there,
Ready and able to help us when we called.
When we hide our tears because we're all grown up now
And not supposed to let life get to us,
He is still there, ready to hold our hand and steady our
    feet
As we continue on this journey of life.
And when we feel so happy we practically burst,
He is there, still ready to hold our hand and rejoice with
    us
As we continue this journey called life.

Do you ever feel lonely? Do you feel like you missed out on half of childhood—or more—because your parents divorced? Do you wish your dad could have restrained himself instead of hurting your mom? Do you wish your mom had been able to make her love last a lifetime? Do you worry about your own marriage and the future of your own children? Do you wish you had someone to talk to who would really understand? Do you feel as though you're sometimes facing it all alone? Friend, please take to heart these words: You are not alone. You have a Father, and he will always be there for you.

Why not pause a moment now to check that out for yourself, to pray and thank God for listening. I'm certain you'll find him there, because Jesus promised long ago, "Surely I am with you always, to the very end of the age" (Matt. 28:20). Go ahead and pray right now. Don't worry, I'll still be here when you're done.

Finished with your prayer? Then let's move on.

Your Father Is Always Active in Your Life

My wife's father, Norm Wakefield, is the kind of in-law most people only dream about. He's a fine man of God who is dedicated to his faith and to his family. Although he lives a few hundred miles away in Arizona, he makes it a point to come out to Colorado to visit us at least once a year. Those visits are always great fun, filled with plenty of laughter and embracing. But if you were to come along with Norm this next summer and stay a few weeks with us all, you'd notice something right away. Norm is always busy.

When he comes, he throws himself into all kinds of household repair projects that will make life easier for me and my family. Here's a short list of things he did last summer: installed a garage door opener, installed a doggie door to the backyard, rewired a light fixture, framed and drywalled the space around our heater, made a screen door from scratch, built doggie steps to go with the doggie door, and more! Whenever he is here, the man is always—cheerfully—at work to make our lives better.

With Norm, however, his work doesn't stop when he leaves our house. He calls and e-mails to check on us every week. He sends us encouraging notes; he prays for us; he explains how to fix things over the phone; he shares his wisdom and advice on life whenever we ask him. He's even been known to unexpectedly donate a few dollars to the "family cause" here in Colorado.

In short, even when we can't see him, he's at work in our lives.

Aaaah, you know where I'm going, don't you? When I look at Norm's involvement in my life, I see a beautiful example of what my heavenly Father is doing day in and day out. I discover that even when I can't see him, he's always at work in my life. In fact God is infinitely more involved in my life than Norm could ever be. My trouble is that I'm often too shortsighted to remember that and start to panic when I can't see his presence impacting my daily realities.

When I read the Scriptures, I notice that I'm not the only one who suffers at times from that kind of shortsightedness. Gehazi, the servant of Elisha the prophet, also had difficulty noticing God's work in his life. His story is recorded in 2 Kings 6:8–23.

It seems that Gehazi's master, Elisha, had been causing trouble for the king of Aram. The king was at war with Israel, and every time he tried to set a trap for his enemies, Elisha interfered. Given a supernatural knowledge of what tactics the king of Aram was pursuing, Elisha would always warn the leaders of Israel, telling them the exact location of Aram's armies. This went on for months. The Bible reports, "Time and again Elisha warned the king [of Israel], so that he was on his guard in such places" (v. 10).

The king of Aram was (understandably) furious! At first he thought he had a spy among his advisors, but soon he discovered that Elisha was actually the spy—even though he was living in a place called Dothan that was nowhere near Aram. Being a man of action, the enemy king promptly sent his troops to Dothan to root out this troublesome adversary. Chariots, horses, and soldiers surrounded the city during the night, intent on capturing or killing Elisha.

The next morning, Elisha's servant, Gehazi, went out to do his early day tasks—and discovered an army bent on killing his master! With great fear and trembling, he raced back to Elisha, told him the situation, and cried, "Oh, my lord, what shall we do?"

Reading the Scripture at this point, you almost get the feeling that Elisha might have yawned, stretched a bit in his chair, and smiled. Terror stood just outside his door, but he was as calm as a placid pond. You see, he knew something Gehazi didn't know: God was at work in his life.

"Don't be afraid," Elisha answered. "Those who are with us are more than those who are with them."

Now, if I'd been Gehazi at that point, I'd have thought my master had flipped his lid. Prophet or no, he had to be truly bonkers to be so lackadaisical about an *army* that had come to capture him.

Then Elisha turned from Gehazi and toward God. "O LORD," he prayed, "open his eyes so he may see."

And suddenly Gehazi saw thousands of angels spread out over the countryside with horses and chariots of fire. Of course he didn't need to worry! God had sent his own army to defend his children—Gehazi just hadn't been able to see it.

Admit it, now. You—like me—are more like Gehazi than Elisha. And you—like me—are often tempted to think God has given up on you, forgotten you, moved to a new address or something, because you just don't see him working in your life.

Maybe it's time that you—and I—take a lesson from Gehazi and remember that even when we can't see him, our heavenly Father is still at work in our lives.

Now, one more thing before we close this chapter. I think it's important for you to know that your Father is waiting for you.

Your Father Is Waiting for You

In his wonderful book *Choosing to Live the Blessing*, John Trent shares a powerful story about his father.[1] John was a junior on his high school football team the first time he heard from his father. John's father, Joe, had left his family when his son was two months old. Years later John found a picture of a man in a military uniform.

"Who's this?" he asked his mother, Zoa.

"It's your dad," she informed him, telling John his dad had once won a medal for bravery during the battle of Guadalcanal.

From that day on John dreamed about meeting his father, about talking with this hero and having him in his own life as well. Finally, when John and his twin brother were in the eleventh grade, Joe Trent called his family.

"Zoa, this is Joe," the hero on the line said. Then, without apologizing or even acknowledging his years of absence in his family's life, he mentioned that he'd read about his sons' football accomplishments in the newspaper. Since he lived near the stadium, he wanted to know if he could come meet the boys after one of their football games.

So the arrangements were made. They would meet on the football field after the next game. John remembers, "The night before the game I hardly slept. . . . he was coming to watch us play. The day of the game I thought about little else."

The home team lost that night, but John wasn't disappointed. He knew he'd played his heart out for his dad. At game's end, John and his brother, still sweating from the night's activities, waited on the field. Their mother joined them. Earnestly they peered into the stands to catch a glimpse of the man they were to meet, the war hero who was their dad.

He never came. John's father had changed his mind and skipped the game, skipping out on his sons' lives once again.

Unfortunately, too many of us who are children of divorce have felt the same kind of disappointment that John and his brother felt that night. We grow weary of part-time parents and we long for a father or mother to return to our daily life. But it doesn't happen. We grow into adulthood and hope that now we can also grow to know our parents. But it doesn't happen. We wait for the opportunities to bring our personal family heroes into our world, and they never come. We, like John, are left only with the thought of what might have been.

What we sometimes miss, however, is that we are often more like Joe Trent than like John Trent. You see, while we are waiting for a father or mother to blow back into our lives, our heavenly Father is waiting for us. While we are longing for a deeper relationship with our parents, our heavenly Father is longing for a deeper relationship with us, waiting for us to open our lives, our days, our every moment to him, waiting to be the Father we turn to in joy and sorrow—and every time in between—waiting to be the Hero who will never fail us, never abandon us.

God is waiting for me, and he's waiting for you. Listen to these promises sampled from Scripture:

> Here I am! I stand at the door and knock. If anyone hears my voice and opens the door, I will come in and eat with him, and he with me.
>
> Revelation. 3:20

> Come near to God and he will come near to you.
>
> James 4:8

> Come to Me, all you who labor and are heavy laden, and I will give you rest.
>
> Matthew 11:28 NKJV

> Be strong and courageous. Do not be afraid or terrified because of them, for the LORD your God goes with you; he will never leave you nor forsake you.
>
> Deuteronomy 31:6

It seems that the familiar question fits here: "If God feels far away, guess who moved?" That's right, it's you. You may have a limited relationship with your earthly parents, but the good news is that your relationship with God doesn't have to be that way. He is there, he is active, and he is waiting for you.

Perhaps now is a good time to end the wait.

Something to Think About . . .

Use the following questions either by yourself or with a group to process what you've learned in this chapter.

- What went through your mind as you read this chapter? What does that tell you about yourself and your relationship with your heavenly Father?
- What keeps you from noticing God's active presence in your life? What can you do about that this week?
- How does it make you feel to know that God waits for you? How can you best respond to that feeling?
- What's one thing you've learned in this chapter that you want to share with someone else? With whom will you share it this week?

Something to Do

On several Post-It notes, write the words "God is here. God is active. God is waiting for me." Place these notes in conspicuous places where you'll see them often this week. For example, stick one on your bathroom mirror, on the refrigerator, by the phone, on your appointment calendar, on your desk at work, on your spouse's forehead (well, maybe not your spouse's forehead, but you get the idea). Each time you see a note, offer a brief "check-in" prayer, asking God to help you grow closer to him, your heavenly Father.

2

A Father Who
Loves You

If someone loves a flower, of which just one single blossom grows in all the millions and millions of stars, it is enough to make him happy just to look at the stars. He can say to himself: Somewhere, my flower is there.

Antoine de Saint-Exupéry, *The Little Prince*

Hidden away on asteroid B-612, according to French author Antoine de Saint-Exupéry, there is a certain flower, a very special flower, in fact. What makes her special is not that she lives on a planet that's no bigger than a house, nor even that she has four bright thorns with which to fight any manner of tigers that may appear. (But, of course, there are no tigers on asteroid B-612, only a few caterpillars and butterflies if the truth be told.) It's not the beauty of her petals, the sweet fragrance of her perfume, nor that, by miraculous coincidence, she was born at exactly the same moment as the sunrise.

What makes this flower special is that she is loved by a boy—a Little Prince, as it were. It is for her that his heart beats, for her that he dutifully waters and shades, cleans out the little volcanoes on his planet, and uproots the nasty baobab sprouts that threaten to crowd her out of the soil. It's for her that he smiles and admires her beauty (overlooking her obvious vanity and selfishness in the process), listens to her childish prattle with undivided interest, and for her that he worries about things like sheep and tigers who may accidentally overrun his precious flower.

Does the Little Prince have to love this flower? Of course not! She is a temporary thing, demanding, vain, insensitive, and even sometimes hurtful. In time, she will disappear without a trace, and no one will miss her in the least—except the Little Prince. In fact he misses her already, longs for her presence (thorns and all!), simply because it is she that he has chosen to love.

Now, I've never met this Little Prince, but I have met a great King who loves me like that boy loves his flower. You see, even when I am a prattling bundle of ludicrous vanity, God my Father smiles down on me, hanging on my every word, rooting out a baobab of sin in my life, watering my life with his love, shielding my ignorance from the winds of doubt and depression. Is it because I deserve to be loved like this? Of course not! I too am a temporary thing, vain, demanding, and often hurtful in my dealings with him and others.

Yet, in spite of who I am and what I do, I am loved. God loves me. My Father loves me with an unquenchable love that doesn't simply affect me, it defines me. And here's the good news: Your heavenly Father loves you that way too.

Your Father's Love Is Fierce

Through my work as president of Nappaland Communications Inc. (a small media company), I have occasionally had unique opportunities to interview popular Christian music artists. A few years ago, I sat with Michael W. Smith, talking about his work, ministry, and what's really important in life. As we were nearing the end of the interview, I asked Michael what he thought was *the most important* thing for people to know about God. Here's what he said: "That [God] loves them unconditionally."

I have to admit, at that point I smiled and nodded at Michael, but inside (where no one could see) I rolled my eyes and said to myself, *How trite is that? Surely the guy who writes such powerful lyrics about Christ could come up with something better than a basic "God loves you" truth to share.*

But he continued, "I think the biggest problem that we have is . . . we don't believe [that God loves us]. And I think that if we would believe it, we'd see great things happen. *I struggle with believing it.* I struggle with believing that there's a never-ending pool of grace that I could never run out of . . . that he really loves me *that much.*"

I finished the interview, shook Michael's hand, and we both went on our merry ways. Now, several years later, I'm still mulling over those words that I thought were so trite back then. Does God really love me *that much?* And do I really believe that can be true?

My experience with my own father's love is no help for me as I wrestle with this thought. One of my earliest memories happened when I was three years old. I was playing with a toy— I think a Winnie the Pooh stuffed bear—and Mom called me to the front porch.

"Come say good-bye to your father," she said matter-of-factly. "He's not going to live here anymore." My three sisters and I gathered on the porch and slowly waved farewell as Dad drove down our driveway and, for all practical purposes, out of our lives.

My father moved to a small town about forty-five minutes away and continued to work near where I lived, but we had only rare contact over the next dozen years. A brief holiday visit, an occasional meeting—for most of my growing-up years my father was an acquaintance, like the mail carrier or the clerk at the grocery store. When I reached high school age, I began to think more about this lack of relationship with my father, and I decided to do something about it.

I lived a few miles from his work, so I decided that once a week or so I'd stop into his office for a visit—no agenda, just drop in and say hi. I knew his supervisors didn't mind brief family visits, so I screwed up my courage and marched in.

Every visit was the same. He greeted me warmly, but he seemed anxious about my being there. I'd ask about his work or try to make small talk. He'd snap his fingers nervously, attempt a lame joke, then walk me to the door. This wasn't working.

Since my grandparents lived near him, any time I visited them, I stopped by Dad's home. Again, he was cordial, but I always seemed to be intruding on his plans.

Finally, one day I sat on the army-cot bed in his one bedroom efficiency and asked him point-blank, "Dad, do you love me?"

There was a pause, then he mumbled, "Your mother says I don't know how to love."

"I don't care what my mother says. I just want to know if you love me."

He paused again, shrugged his shoulders, and said, "I guess I don't know how to love."

After that, I quit trying to be part of my father's life. For the next near-decade I lived with the assumption that my father really didn't love me, his only son.[1]

My father passed away not long ago, and at the time of his death he still had not said, "I love you," to me, his child. To be fair, I don't recall ever saying it to him either. But unlike my father (or me, for that matter), God whispers those words to me continually—in the breeze that slips over my face in summer, in the smile that wraps my heart around my own son's finger, in the quiet of prayer and praise, in the words of his holy Book, and in thousands of other ways I can barely recognize or even imagine.

And now, years after my little twenty-minute interview with Michael W. Smith, I have learned something about that which the singer hinted at, and which overwhelms me with its simplicity and power: God loves me *that much.*

You see, God's love for you and me is not frail or temporary, able to be wounded by divorce or unkind words or even legal proceedings. Unlike my earthly father's love, God's love for me is *fierce.* It's a fighting love, determined to overcome any obstacle that gets in its way. It is the epitome of "tough love," because it will not be denied, will not allow anything at all to interfere with its passion and grace for me.

Don't believe it? I admit I have trouble believing it too. It seems too good to be true! But just listen to how the apostle Paul described this fierce, fighting love of God for us:

> Who shall separate us from the love of Christ?
> Shall tribulation,
> or distress,
> or persecution,
> or famine,
> or nakedness,
> or danger,
> or sword?
> . . . No, in all these things we are more than conquerors
> through him who loved us.
> For I am sure that
> neither death
> nor life,
> nor angels
> nor rulers,
> nor things present
> nor things to come,
> nor powers,
> nor height

nor depth,
nor anything else in all creation,
will be able to separate us from the love of God in Christ
Jesus our Lord.

Romans 8:35–39 ESV

Wow! That about covers every possibility, doesn't it?

Do you realize what Paul is saying here? Nothing—absolutely nothing—can ever overcome God's fierce love for you, can ever make him give up on loving you, can ever limit his all-powerful affection for you.

Did you happen to get mad and curse God today? He still loves you. Did you do something that fills you with shame and regret, something you know God despises? Your Father still loves you. Did you fail miserably at a job or relationship or in the face of temptation? Read the words again: God loves you, and he loves you with a fierceness that makes a hurricane seem like a splash in a baby's bathtub. His love for you is a force that will not—cannot!—be denied. So get over your disbelief on this one. Sometimes things that seem too good to be true are simply good because they are true. Such is the way of God's fighting love for you.

Your Father's Love Is Unrelenting

And that leads us to this next truth you must know about God. Your Father's love for you is unrelenting, unwavering, unstoppable. How can that be, you ask? How can the love of anyone—even God—never wane in its intensity, at least from time to time?

The answer is one you must understand, for it defines more than who you are, it dictates the reality in which you live. You see, God doesn't love you because you are a "good" person; he doesn't love you because he is obligated to (God is not "obligated" to anyone or anything!); he doesn't love you because of what you've done or even for who you are. God loves you because of who *he* is—your Father.

This is the choice that your adoptive heavenly Father has made concerning you—to love you with an unrelenting fervor, with a love that doesn't fade and has no need of increasing, with a love that gladly sacrifices all to continue its pursuit of you.

I was an adult when I discovered the classic children's book *The Runaway Bunny* by Margaret Wise Brown. In this delightful tale, the mother of a brash little rabbit hears her child announce one day, "I am running away."

The mother is unfazed. She says simply, "If you run away, I will run after you. For you are my little bunny."

The would-be runaway isn't so easily stymied, however. He announces that if she runs after him, he will turn into a fish and swim away in a stream. Says the mother, "If you become a fish in a trout stream, I will become a fisherman and I will fish for you."

And so it goes. The little bunny says he will become a rock on a mountain, a flower in a hidden garden, a bird, a sailboat, and more. And for each new obstacle, the mother bunny has a plan, promising to pursue her child as a mountain climber, a gardener, a tree for resting birds, the wind in a sailboat's sails, and so on.

Finally, the runaway bunny realizes that nothing he can do will enable him to slip away from the relentless love of his mother. "Shucks," he says at the end of the story, "I might just as well stay where I am and be your little bunny."[2]

Friend, that mama bunny is a beautiful picture of how God's relentless love pursues you and me! No matter where we may try to run from our Father's love, no matter what tactics we invent to shield ourselves from his embrace, no matter what circumstances in life threaten to separate us from him, God's love never wanes, never fades, never flickers or dims. His is a relentless, unwavering love that pursues us over hill and dale, under the shadows of sadness, and in the sunshine of joy. Like that mother bunny, our Father will always, *always* come after us.

Forgive me for appealing to comedy at this point, but I can't help myself. *Pee-Wee's Big Adventure* is a silly movie with little substance beyond its ability to make us laugh (which, for me at least, is plenty!). But there is one scene I find amusingly insightful.[3]

Our hero, Pee-Wee Herman (played by Paul Reubens), is on a cross-country quest to reclaim his precious, stolen bicycle. Along the way, he ends up at a truck stop/diner/prehistoric museum and gift shop (really, it all makes sense in the movie . . . sort of!). At any rate, it's here that Pee-Wee meets a kind waitress named Simone (portrayed by Diane Salinger). After her shift, the two of them walk out to a gigantic dinosaur sculpture to talk the night away. The dinosaur is hollow, with stairs inside that lead to a quiet bench with a view of the night sky (seen through the T-rex's plastic eyes).

Eventually Pee-Wee asks Simone what her greatest desire is in life.

"I want to live in the city of eternal love, Paris," she replies dreamily.

Our young hero asks what's keeping Simone from living out her dream. She then tells him about her boyfriend, Andy, a big, meaty bull of a man who flunked high school French class and now would never allow her to go there.

Cut to the door outside the plastic dinosaur, and there, listening in with a jealous intensity is none other than Andy himself!

Back to Pee-Wee and Simone.

"Simone," the young man says earnestly, "this is your dream. You have to follow it!"

"I know you're right," the waitress starts, "but . . . "

"But what?" Pee-Wee interrupts, unaware that Andy is just outside the door, hanging on his every word. "Everyone

I know has a big 'but'! C'mon, Simone, let's talk about your big 'but.'"

Outside the door, Andy's jealous mind misinterprets the conversation, and (as usually happens in movies like this) comic endangerment ensues.

Of course, the humor in this scene is in the misunderstanding of the homonyms, *but* and, well, a common word for the human derriere. However, I tell you this story not to make you chuckle (okay, maybe to make you smile a bit) but primarily because it reminds me that we children of divorce often carry along "a big 'but'" that can hinder our ability to receive the love God wants to lavish on us!

It's like a situation I read about in an interesting book called *The Unexpected Legacy of Divorce* by Judith Wallerstein and others. This book is the result of a twenty-five-year study on children of divorce. Wallerstein and her colleagues followed a specific group of children whose parents divorced in the 1970s through the 1990s. It was only near the end of this study that this researcher finally realized that a childhood in a divorced home affects more than just adolescence. She says, "We have not fully appreciated how divorce continues to shape the lives of young people after they reach full adulthood . . . about their intimate feelings, the major turning points in their lives, how they made the choices they did."[4]

One of Wallerstein's subjects, Karen James, understands something of that, though. Her parents divorced when she was ten years old, and twenty-four years later (at the age of thirty-four) she was just beginning to understand how that influenced her daily attitudes and decisions.

After falling in love with the man of her dreams, she found herself inexplicably hesitant when he proposed marriage to her. The affirmation of his love for her in this way should have made her blissfully happy. Instead it frightened her. Listen to how she describes it:

You see, [my parents' divorce is] not all behind me. Part of me is always waiting for disaster to strike. I keep reminding myself that I'm doing this to myself, but the truth is that I live in dread that something bad will happen to me. Some terrible loss will change my life, and it only gets worse as things get better for me. Maybe that's the permanent result of my parents' divorce. Gavin [my fiancé] says I'm always waiting for the other shoe to drop. I've learned to contain it. I no longer wake up in terror when I go to sleep happy, but this feeling does not ever go away.[5]

Karen's experience has been repeated millions of times in the lives of other children of divorce—and has probably been a part of your life as well. In short, Ms. James is telling us what Pee-Wee Herman told us—a bit less eloquently: We children of divorce have all got "a big but." Intellectually we can accept that God loves us, but in our heart we're still waiting for the catch, for the accompanying disaster, for that "other shoe to drop."

Okay, God loves me. But what about my failures? What about the hardships in my life? What about . . . ?

Sure, my Father loves me. But sooner or later he's going to leave me just like my dad/mom/friend did.

I'm glad God loves me today. But will he still love me tomorrow?

I want to believe my Father loves me, but _____ (you fill in the blank here).

Friend, it's time we got over our big "buts"! Here is the truth: Your Father loves you, with an unrelenting fierceness that lasts both now and forever.

The teachings of Jesus revealed this truth for me in a way no other teacher could. Speaking to a crowd of people, he found himself surrounded by both the esteemed and despised members of society—from the cheating, lawless tax collectors to Pharisees, the highly regarded religious leaders of that day. In that context, he began to tell stories about God and the relentlessness of his love.

The first story was about a man with one hundred sheep (Luke 15:1–7). He is a shepherd who is out in the fields caring for his flock when suddenly he discovers one lamb is missing. What does that shepherd do? Jesus says that immediately he leaves the ninety-nine others to "go after the one that is lost, *until he finds it.* And when he finds it, he lays it on his shoulders, rejoicing" (v. 5 ESV; italics mine).

The second story Christ told was about a woman with ten valuable coins (vv. 8–10). Unexpectedly she discovers that one coin is missing. What will she do? According to Jesus, she will immediately "light a lamp and sweep the house and seek diligently *until she finds it*" (v. 8 ESV; italics mine). Nothing will keep her from finding that coin!

The third story is probably the most famous. It is the tale of a father and his wayward son (vv. 11–32). The son takes leave of the father's home and safety and very presence. He runs away to faraway lands and squanders his wealth and health on wine, women, and wild living. Finally he hits rock bottom, finding himself reduced to feeding pigs for a living— and wishing he could eat the pig slop in his bucket. In disgrace he returns home, expecting to be shunned and forgotten. Instead, he discovers his father has never given up hope that his son would return, looking each day for any sign of his son from afar. And as he falls weeping into his father's arms, he learns that the father's love is still as strong on this day of homecoming as it was the day the foolish boy left in the first place.

A shepherd, a woman who owns valuable coins, and a father. All three are pictures of Someone else, of your Father who loves you relentlessly, of God who searches for you like a shepherd climbing the hills to find a lost sheep and rejoices over finding you like a woman who's recovered a great treasure or like a father who never gives up hope that his son will one day come home.

Friend, you can run but (thank God) you can never hide from God's unwavering, unstoppable love for you. Amen to that!

Your Father's Love Is *Not* . . .

No discussion of this relentless love of God is complete without taking note of what our Father's love is *not*. Too often his love toward us has been masked and marred by our fallible humanity, and we need to be reminded that what we see is not always what is true. So, before I end this chapter, let me briefly say:

> *Your Father's love is not a pendulum* that swings back and forth between love and disgust, depending on how "good" you are each day (see Rom. 5:8).
>
> *Your Father's love is not open to your approval or acceptance.* God loves you whether you like it or not (see Rom. 8:38–39).
>
> *Your Father's love is not temporary,* like a battery that runs down or a divorced father whose affection for you is limited by his weekend visitation rights. His love for you is just as strong and ever present today as it was yesterday, as it was two thousand years ago, as it will be ten thousand years from now (see Jer. 31:3).
>
> *Your Father's love is not harsh toward you.* He's not "out to get you" or waiting gleefully for the slightest opportunity to "teach you a lesson" every time you make a mistake. His love is patient, kind, keeps no record of your wrongs, and so much more! (see 1 Cor. 13:4–7 and 1 John 4:8).

Your Father's love is not a secret. If you feel unloved by God, it's not his fault—it is your own. If you refuse to bask in the wonder of God's love for you, it's not your Father's fault; it's still your own. His love for you is repeated daily in the wind, in your soul, and in the person of Jesus Christ (see 1 John 4:9–10).

As I close this chapter, I can't think of any way to say this more plainly. *Your Father loves you.* Your Father's love for you cannot be dimmed by your actions, your failures, your attitudes, your circumstances, your doubts, your emotions, your anything.

And if you should happen to find yourself feeling far away from your Father's love, be assured of this—he will always come after you, ready and willing to wrap you up in his grand embrace so that together the two of you may dry your tears and stand ready to face whatever may come.

Something to Think About . . .

Use the following questions either by yourself or with a group to process what you've learned in this chapter.

- When have you felt, unmistakably, God's love for you? Describe that time.
- Do you find it difficult to believe, as Michael W. Smith says, that God loves *you* unconditionally? Why or why not?
- What are the "big buts" that keep you from fully enjoying God's love for you?
- What would you add to the list of things that God's love is *not?*

Something to Do

Buy a little plastic ring from a gum ball machine at your local grocery or discount store and put it on a chain necklace. Wear the necklace/ring underneath your shirt for one whole day. Each time you notice the ring during the day, let it be a reminder to you of this truth: *Your Father loves you!*

3

A Father Who Understands You

In his classic satirical work *The Devil's Dictionary*, Ambrose Bierce offered this profound definition of the term *understanding:*

> *Understanding, n.* A cerebral secretion that enables one having it to know a house from a horse by the roof on the house. Its nature and laws have been exhaustively expounded by Locke, who rode a house, and Kant, who lived in a horse.[1]

Of course we chuckle at the humor apparent in Bierce's definition, but the truth is we are often locked into an existence of misunderstanding as we go through this life each day. Well, at least I am! At the time of this writing, I've been married for more than fifteen years to my wife, Amy. After that much time together, I've discovered Amy to be a wonderful woman—compassionate, intelligent, creative, talented, inspiring, and more.

I've also discovered that I'll never understand this woman who shares my home! I suspect that most men feel the same way. In fact I recently made a "top ten list" of things husbands can't seem to understand about their wives. Let me share it with you now:

Top Ten Things Husbands Don't Understand about Their Wives

1. Why when she's wrong, and he's right, he's still wrong anyway.
2. Why the quickest way to make her change her mind is simply to take her side in the argument.
3. Why she'll weep with joy at a romantic movie but growl in annoyance when he tries to interrupt with a kiss her daily reading of the newspaper.
4. Why she pines for "time alone" then spends it all in the company of her sisters.
5. Why she can remember who won the Academy Award for best supporting actress on her thirteenth birthday but can't recall which side is offense and which is defense during a big football game.
6. How she manages to look just as stunning in sweats and old T-shirts while washing the car as she does in dressy outfits when heading off to work (not that he minds, of course).
7. How she knows just when he needs a good foot rub or cup of hot cocoa.
8. Why she can't resist watching scary movies even though it means he'll have to escort her to the bathroom at midnight for at least a week after.
9. How her smile can make him feel like a king, and her tears can make him certain he's merely a fool.
10. Why a woman as intelligent as she chose to marry a lunkhead like him.

Fortunately, we husbands are not alone in our misunderstandings of this world. An inability to grasp the obvious is so prevalent in our lawsuit-happy society that it has resulted in a proliferation of absurd "warning labels" attached to every product imaginable.

For instance, I read recently about a fireplace log that had this warning prominently displayed on it: "Caution—Risk of Fire." A box of birthday candles strongly advised the consumer: "Do NOT use soft wax as earplugs or for any other function that involves insertion into a body cavity." Then there's the manufacturer that, for reasons yet unknown, emblazoned this warning notice on its CD players: "Do not use the Ultradisk2000 as a projectile in a catapult."[2]

The fact that anyone might confuse a CD with catapult ammunition seems to indicate that we have a serious problem understanding this world and the people who live in it! And that general lack of understanding has contributed to the difficulties you and I have today.

You see, our parents had no real idea how their divorce would affect us for the rest of our lives. Sure, they tried to understand what we might go through, and I'm confident they did their best. But no amount of human wisdom could predict the true hurt they were causing their children; no glimpse into our young faces could truly reveal the scars we would carry into adulthood.

In spite of their best efforts, they just didn't understand.

But God does. He always has, and he always will. And we can take comfort in that.

Your Father Knows It All

There is no limit to your heavenly Father's understanding. No wisdom is too great for him, no knowledge too confusing, no emotion too foreign, no fact too obscure, no feeling too hidden, no plan too complex, no science too microscopic, no history unheard of, no nothing! God doesn't simply *know* all, like a computer that stores billions of bits of facts, your Father *understands* all, knows the greatest and least details with equal intimacy, and understands the whos and whats and wheres and whens and whys and hows behind them all.

Don't believe me? Listen to what the Bible has to say about it in the poetry of Psalm 139:1–18:

> O LORD, you have searched me
>   and you know me.
> You know when I sit and when I rise;
>   you perceive my thoughts from afar.
> You discern my going out and my lying down;
>   you are familiar with all my ways.
> Before a word is on my tongue
>   you know it completely, O LORD.
> You hem me in—behind and before;
>   you have laid your hand upon me.
> Such knowledge is too wonderful for me,
>   too lofty for me to attain.
> Where can I go from your Spirit?
>   Where can I flee from your presence?
> If I go up to the heavens, you are there;
>   if I make my bed in the depths, you are there.
> If I rise on the wings of the dawn,
>   if I settle on the far side of the sea,
> even there your hand will guide me,
>   your right hand will hold me fast.
> If I say, "Surely the darkness will hide me
>   and the light become night around me,"
> even the darkness will not be dark to you;
>   the night will shine like the day,
>   for darkness is as light to you.
> For you created my inmost being;
>   you knit me together in my mother's womb.
> I praise you because I am fearfully and
>   wonderfully made;

your works are wonderful,
I know that full well.
My frame was not hidden from you
when I was made in the secret place.
When I was woven together in the depths of the earth,
your eyes saw my unformed body.
All the days ordained for me
were written in your book
before one of them came to be.
How precious to me are your thoughts, O God!
How vast is the sum of them!
Were I to count them,
they would outnumber the grains of sand.
When I awake,
I am still with you.

Tonight I joined several friends from my church in a small group meeting. As is our custom, we spent the first hour or so sharing our concerns and then praying about them. This time was more sober than many.

Early on, one woman spoke. "My cousin Seldon[3] was feeling ill this week, so he went to the doctor for a checkup. They discovered cancer so far developed that they're not even going to treat it. Now he's just waiting to die."

Moments later another spoke. "A woman I work with recently found out she is pregnant. She is a single mom with two preschool children already. Unfortunately, because of a heart condition she has, her last pregnancy caused her to have a stroke that almost killed her. Her doctors are telling her that if she carries this one to term, there's a 90 percent chance she won't survive. Now she must choose between her own life and the life of her unborn baby."

And so we prayed. It was all we could do, and the best thing we could do. As we were praying I was struck by a thought. We were stunned, surprised, and helpless at the news these two ladies shared. God wasn't. Our heavenly Father wasn't caught off guard in the least bit. In fact he knew about both situations in intimate detail before we even opened our mouths to pray. Not only that, he understood the *why* behind each of these hardships, felt the sorrow of Seldon and this single mother, knew the hope that lies ahead of everyone involved.

We are human. We can never comprehend why a mother must choose between her own life and that of her child. We can't figure out why our parents, who started out a marriage deeply in love, found each other intolerable in later years. We can't even understand why an event that happened in our childhood (our parents' divorce) is something that still holds sway over us today.

But God can and does understand. God not only understands our circumstances, he has a deep, perpetual comprehension of how those circumstances impact each one of us as well. Better yet, he doesn't simply know us, our Father uses his great omniscience on our behalf, day in and day out, every minute we take a breath and beyond.

Theologian A. W. Tozer explains the great knowledge and understanding of God with the life-changing observation that God's limitless wisdom is used to lavish goodness and love onto his children. "In the Holy Scriptures," Tozer says, "wisdom, when used of God . . . always carries a strong moral connotation. It is conceived as being pure, loving, and good. . . .

"Wisdom sees everything in focus, each in proper relation to all, and is thus able to work toward predestined goals with flawless precision. All God's acts are done in perfect wisdom, first for His own glory, and then for the highest good of the greatest number for the longest time."[4]

Here is the point, then. If God knows everything, he must understand you, must know what makes you tick, what brings you joy and sorrow, must understand that your childhood experiences have irretrievably shaped who you are today. Further, he must be using that understanding to come alongside you (and me) to help us walk through the painful and happy days of our lives.

And that, my friend, means we are no longer alone in this world.

Your Father Knows How You Feel

I've been a professional writer for many years now and published dozens of books and hundreds of articles. As I look back on my career, I notice there are some things that are easier for me to write than others. For instance, I stink at writing technical reports. My research-oriented works often take several rounds of rewrites before they are polished enough to print.

There is one subject that is easy for me, though, in both fiction and nonfiction—loneliness. Whenever I'm writing about a character in a story or a real-life person who faces the sorrow of being alone, I seem to get it right the first try. You see, I know what that feels like. I know the colors of that kind of sorrow. I know the smells, the sounds, the awful aching of the chest that comes and goes when you just don't expect it. And so, invariably, I write those scenes easily, in a short amount of time. And invariably those pieces are the ones people send me notes about later.

It strikes me as silly, really. I'm surrounded by people who love me, by family and friends who will come to me at a moment's notice. Yet somewhere in the core of me, there is still a sick child who is sweating in the darkness with fever and nausea, who can't shake the feeling of being alone, knowing that Mom's at work (as usual) and Dad's nowhere within reach. It is that child who makes it so easy for me to write about loneliness and sorrow. I know him. I know what he feels, what he wishes for, and what he won't get no matter how hard he wishes.

There are times when my wife and I will reminisce about our experiences as children. Sometimes I try to explain how I missed having a dad around to do things like teach me to shave or throw a football in the yard. She nods in agreement and says, "I know just how you feel! When I was a teenager, my dad used to go on trips to speak at churches or camps and stuff. It used to make me mad that he'd leave on those trips so much because I didn't like him to be gone for long."

Then I will smile and nod and change the subject because inside I am thinking, *No, Amy, you don't understand. There's no way you can understand. Your father always came home. Mine never did.*

Social scientist Judith Wallerstein and her coauthors shed some light on this in their discussion of the way divorce wreaks emotional havoc on children.

> The first upheaval occurs at breakup. Children are frightened and angry, terrified of being abandoned by both parents, and they feel responsible for the divorce. Most children are taken by surprise; few are relieved. As adults, they remember with sorrow and anger how little support they got from their parents when it happened. They recall how they were expected to adjust overnight to a terrifying number of changes that confounded them. Even children who had seen or heard violence at home made no connection between the violence and the decision to divorce. The children concluded early on, silently and sadly, that family relationships are fragile and that the tie between a man and woman can break capriciously, without warning. They worried ever after that parent-child relationships are also unreliable and can break any time. These early experiences colored their later expectations. As the postdivorce family took shape, their world increasingly resembled what they feared most. Home was a lonely place . . .[5]

Why do I share this with you now? Two reasons. First, I suspect that what Judith Wallerstein and I have just described is remarkably similar to what you have experienced. As such, it's time one of us brought the subject up and dealt with it. Second, and most important, I want you to know this one never-ending truth: God understands how you feel.

My wife, bless her heart, really does *try* to understand how I feel, but like all humans, her efforts can never measure up. Our heavenly Father, however, *understands.* He knows, first, simply because he is God. If that's not enough for you, then let me remind you that he also knows because he himself has *lived* it.

The Bible reveals in the prophetic passage of Isaiah 53:3–4 a striking description of Jesus Christ, the God-Man who came and lived among us:

> He was despised and rejected by men,
> a man of sorrows, and familiar with suffering.
> Like one from whom men hide their faces
> he was despised, and we esteemed him not.
> Surely he took up our infirmities
> and carried our sorrows,
> yet we considered him stricken by God,
> smitten by him, and afflicted.

Do you hear what this passage is saying to your heart? God knows how you feel. He is a man of sorrows. He is well acquainted with grief—your grief. He has borne the sorrow of solitude and rejection. And best of all, if you will let him, he will carry your sorrows too.

One thing I have discovered about grief is this: It never truly ends. Sure, we learn to put it aside, to forget about it and get on with life. But suddenly, in the most unexpected moments, that white-hot flash of sorrow reminds us of the moments of loss. That sadness will fade, but it never goes completely away. And honestly, that's okay. The feelings of loss we experienced as children are part of who we are. They are nothing to be ashamed of or repressed.

Yet, in those quiet moments when the loneliness hits— and sometimes it comes even in the midst of a crowded room—it's nice to know our Father has felt those emotions too. We can be comforted by his spiritual embrace, strengthened by knowing that he can empathize with this deep, often hidden feeling.

We are not alone.

Our Father understands.

And that makes all the difference.

Your Father Knows Your True Worth

For years—decades even—Wil Townsend[6] refused to part with a dusty old baseball he kept hidden in a room in his house. It had originally been a present to Wil from a kind uncle. With its hard casing and sewn-in core, Wil's baseball was not much different from any other of the thousands of baseballs made and played with each year.

Unlike other ones, though, this ball never experienced the joy of being smacked into oblivion by a gum-chewing ten-year-old. It never got tossed around in the yard or rolled down a street or pitched at bottles in a state fair. Wil never even found the right time to pull out the old ball and slap it in a glove once or twice.

To be honest, Wil's baseball was mostly useless, just a forgotten fixture taking up space in the Townsend home. And there it stayed for five years, ten, twenty years, and more.

One day Wil's wife, Dorothy, discovered the old ball, wrapped in tissues in a long-forgotten storage space. She showed it to a family friend of theirs who was something of a collector, and his jaw dropped. Inked across the lining of the ball was a much-treasured autograph of baseball great Mickey Mantle.

Wil and Dorothy had kept the ball safe and protected for years because they knew that one little ink spot made by a baseball legend made that ball more valuable than hundreds of brand-new baseballs in a local store. In fact, when they finally sold it, the Mantle-autographed ball garnered a whopping one thousand dollars!

I've got to tell you, over the years of my life, I've often felt like a forgotten old baseball—and I think you probably have too. We who, as children, have lived through the loss of a parent can't help but feel abandoned or of little value from time to time. But the truth is, regardless of the status of our parents' marriage, regardless of the lack of investment one or both of our parents may have made in our life, we carry a value far greater than ten thousand Mickey Mantle–signed baseballs. We bear the signature of Father God etched across our heart and soul; the handcrafted mark of the Creator of all declares the priceless worth our Father places on each one of us.

Trouble is we often have a hard time believing we're of great worth, especially when we're feeling depressed or sad or going through a "worthless baseball" moment. When that happens, we become people who believe lies rather than the truth of God's love in our lives. Here's what authors Neil Anderson and Dave Park have to say about this:

> The following statements are some of the most common lies that depressed [people] tend to believe about themselves, life in general and their relationships with God:
>
> > I'm worthless and would be better off dead.
> > I have no value and no meaningful purpose in life.
> > I'll never amount to anything.
> > No one loves me or cares about me.
> > My situation is hopeless. I see no way out but to die.
> > I'm stupid! I'm ugly!
> > I'm a mistake!
> > God doesn't love me and He won't help me.
> > Life is the pits.
> > My future is hopeless.
> > Nobody can help me.

The list could continue with many other blasphemous thoughts about God and negative thoughts about the [people] themselves and others.

Nobody is going to fix the past. Not even God will do that. Nevertheless, the gospel assures us that *we can be free from the past because we are not primarily products of the past.* We are primarily products of Christ's work on the cross and His resurrection. Our primary identity is no longer in the flesh; it is in Christ.[7]

The Bible backs up what Anderson and Park are telling us. Jesus impressed this on his disciples in Luke 12:6–7 (NLT): "What is the price of five sparrows? A couple of pennies? Yet God does not forget a single one of them. And the very hairs on your head are all numbered. So don't be afraid; you are more valuable to him than a whole flock of sparrows."

Your Father knows your true worth—and it's more than you can ever imagine! Your parents may or may not have had an inkling as to the value of the child they conceived and brought into this world, but your Father does. He understands more than anyone what Ephesians 2:10 (NLT) declares (italics mine): "*For we are God's masterpiece.* He has created us anew in Christ Jesus, so that we can do the good things he planned for us long ago."

Friend, your Father understands you and all you've been through. He knows how you feel, and, perhaps best of all, he knows your true worth. Now, isn't it about time you started taking advantage of that?

Something to Think About . . .

Use the following questions either by yourself or with a group to process what you've learned in this chapter.

- What makes it difficult for you to believe that God understands everything about you?
- How do you handle the "secret sorrow" that most children of divorce experience, even after they've become adults?
- Why do you think it's important to understand that God knows how you feel?
- When are you tempted to devalue your perception of your true worth? What can you do about that?

Something to Do

Tomorrow keep a log that lists all the emotions you feel during the course of the day. At the end of the day, review your list privately and spend some time praying over it, asking God to help you understand why you felt the way you did. Afterward, take a moment to thank your Father for always understanding how you feel—no matter what!

4

A Father Who
Accepts You

T here are moments in a life when everything changes, times when an isolated incident redirects the torrent of casual circumstances into a flood of blessings. Mary Ann Bird experienced one of those moments as a child in Mrs. Leonard's second grade classroom.

"I grew up knowing I was different," Mary Ann says, "and I hated it." Born with a cleft palate—that is, an abnormal separation in the mouth—the child was acutely aware of the fact that her face was not as attractive as other kids'. She remembers, "[I was] a little girl with a misshapen lip, crooked nose, lopsided teeth, and garbled speech."

As is often the case with children who are "different," Mary Ann experienced merciless taunting and teasing from her classmates. When other children asked her, out of morbid curiosity, what had happened to her lip, she often made up an answer, telling them she'd fallen and cut it on a piece of glass. "Somehow it was more acceptable to have suffered an accident than to have been born different," she reasoned.

By the time she was in second grade, Mary Ann reports that she was convinced no one outside her own family ever would, or even could, love her.

Enter Mrs. Leonard. This second grade teacher was "short, round, [and] happy," full of joy and plenty of smiles. Every child in second grade adored her, eagerly seeking her approval and affection.

Once each year the children of Mary Ann's class were required to take a hearing test to gauge whether any of them needed medical attention in that area. The test was simple enough. Students would take turns standing at the door, covering one ear at a time, while the teacher (seated at her desk across the room) would whisper something to the child. The person taking the test would then be required to repeat back to the teacher what he or she had heard.

The previous year the first grade teacher had whispered meaningless phrases like "The sky is blue" and "Do you have new shoes?" So when Mary Ann took her place next to the door, she expected more of the same.

Mrs. Leonard, however, had something else in mind. Looking directly at the "deformed" child across the room, she whispered, "I wish you were my little girl."

As that simple statement echoed in Mary Ann's ears, the unconditional acceptance behind it worked an unseen magic on her heart, transforming the forlorn second grader from an unwanted, unattractive creature into the beautiful, beloved, treasured child she truly was.

"God must have put [those words] into her mouth," Mary Ann commented years later, "those seven words that changed my life."[1]

You Are Always Welcome in Your Father's Arms

Deep within each of us is a need to be accepted, to be welcomed into the life of another, or into a group of others. Moti-

vational speaker and professional sales trainer Dr. Peter
Hirsch describes it this way:

> One of the most powerful values many people share in our
> world today is *belonging.* People want to belong, to be a part
> of what's going on and what's happening . . . and they often
> want us to know who they are and what it is they belong to as
> well. That's another value, which some marketers are now call-
> ing "egonomics." Look at the T-shirts, athletic gear, and hats
> we buy—even if we've never shot a basket, run a mile, or sailed.[2]

This need for belonging is only magnified when a child
feels the spoken or unspoken rejection that comes with a
parental breakup. No matter what Mom or Dad told us, when
one of them moved out, it left you and me feeling as though
that parent had rejected us on at least some level.

Rejection hurts. That's why peer pressure is such a huge
force on young people (and such a dangerously subtle one
on adults). And that's why societal segments form with such
regularity and intensity. The truth is that people will do just
about anything to be accepted.

I read a cartoon not long ago that humorously illustrates
this point. After census researchers announced in 2001 that
fewer than one out of four households in America is made
up of married couples and their children, many people realized that divorce is the unexpected norm for our society.
Political cartoonist Mike Smith satirized this in my local
newspaper. In this particular panel, a couple sits in their car,
with their sullen-faced child riding in the backseat. Both parents look worried, and the mother is saying to the father,
"Billy was trying to fit in at school today. He told everyone
his parents were divorced."[3]

We chuckle at the irony of this silly cartoon, but if we are
honest, little Billy's desire to "fit in" somewhere is something
we've all felt—and continue to feel day in and day out. For
some, that can lead to extreme, violent behavior, like the

youths who shave their heads and adopt radical racist views, or the Columbine High School killers who started a "trench coat mafia" and murdered their classmates because they felt ostracized by others at school.

For others, like Carla Germaine and Greg Cordell, feeling that they don't fit in contributes to a low self-esteem that prompts them to take nearly any risk to become accepted by another. That's why, in 1999, Carla and Greg entered a radio station's lonely hearts contest called "Two Strangers and a Wedding." When they won, that meant they were the two strangers, and the wedding would be theirs. These two lonely hearts were so desperate to be accepted— and loved—by another, that (at the radio station's suggestion) they married each other the first time they met! Perhaps the saddest commentary, however, is that more than two hundred people entered this so-called "contest" to win a spouse.[4]

Why do people act with such neediness as this? And why is that silent desperation so often present in the heart of a child of divorce? It's because we have felt the pain of a parent's perceived rejection and, like Mary Ann Bird, deep down inside we all have a secret desire to hear someone whisper, "I wish you were mine!"

Ready for the good news? There is Someone who is constantly whispering those words of acceptance to you; Someone has promised never to turn you away. Regardless of what you've done or what you've been through, regardless of how you've been hurt or caused hurt to others, you are *always* welcome in your heavenly Father's arms.

What does that mean, exactly? Gladys Hunt gave some insight into that years ago in *Eternity* magazine. Here's how she explained it:

> Acceptance means you are valuable just as you are. It allows you to be the real you. You are not forced into someone else's idea of who you are. It means your ideas are taken seriously since they reflect you. You can talk about how you feel inside,

why you feel that way, and someone really cares. . . . It doesn't mean you'll never be corrected or shown to be wrong. It simply means it's safe to be you and no one will destroy you out of prejudice.[5]

Safe to be you. Exciting, isn't it? God, who knows you better than you know yourself, is also the One who promises it's safe to be you in his presence. Here are just a few Scriptures on this subject (italics mine):

> Then Jesus said, "Come to me, *all of you* who are weary and carry heavy burdens, and I will give you rest."
>
> Matthew 11:28 NLT

> If my father and mother leave me, *the LORD will take me in.*
>
> Psalm 27:10 NCV

> For the LORD your God is a merciful God; *he will not abandon* or destroy you or forget the covenant with your forefathers, which he confirmed to them by oath.
>
> Deuteronomy 4:31

> Those who know your name will trust in you, for *you, LORD, have never forsaken those who seek you.*
>
> Psalm 9:10

> [Jesus said,] "All that the Father gives me will come to me, and *whoever comes to me I will never cast out.*"
>
> John 6:37 ESV

Perhaps a good way to communicate this truth further is by telling a story. This one is about Thomas Jefferson, the third president of the United States.

It seems that one fateful day President Jefferson and a group of companions were riding horseback on a journey across the country when they came to a river that had flooded its banks due to a recent storm. The swirling water ran rough and rugged, threatening to sweep away and drown any who dared to cross it. In fact it had already swept away and destroyed the bridge that had, until the storm, provided a safe passage across.

Finally, it was decided that each man could ford the river on horseback, one at a time, carefully clinging to and directing the strength of the horse underneath him. Near the edge of the water was another man, a stranger, who also needed to cross the river—but who had no horse to help him. As the riders slowly began to cross the raging waters, this stranger looked carefully into the eyes of each man before that man entered the river.

The first rider crossed, and the stranger didn't stop him. The second did the same; still the stranger refused to ask for help. Finally, it was President Jefferson's turn, and the horseless traveler stepped forward.

"Friend," he called out, "would you be willing to ferry me across this river with you?"

The president responded without hesitation, welcoming the stranger onto his horse. After a short but turbulent journey, both were safely on the other side. As the stranger dismounted from Jefferson's horse, another in the group was overcome with curiosity.

"Tell me," he asked, "why did you select the president to ask this favor of?"

The stranger was shocked to hear that the man who'd just ferried him across the river was none other than the president of the United States. Finally, he answered, "All I know is that on some of your faces was written the answer 'no' and on some of them was the answer 'yes.'" The stranger gestured toward Jefferson. "His," he said, "was a 'yes' face."[6]

Please understand this, friend. As you prepare to cross over the raging rivers of this difficult life, God is continually gazing your way, and his is a "yes" face! When you need more than a friend, more than family, turn your eyes toward him. Your Father is waiting, always ready to welcome you into his arms.

For Your Father, Acceptance Equals Adoption

Perhaps the reason God always wears a "yes" face toward us is because we never come to him as strangers. When our heavenly Father sees us coming, he sees *his child*. Thanks to Jesus Christ, God's unconditional acceptance means more than just being allowed into heaven. It means being welcomed into the family!

To put it more plainly, then, for God, acceptance equals adoption. When your Father chose to accept you, he chose to adopt you, to make you his precious, beloved child.

Neil Anderson explains this further in his valuable book, *Who I Am in Christ.*

> Our heavenly father didn't *need* us, but he *wanted* us. This unconditional love and acceptance of God is the essential foundation for our holy living. . . . There are no illegitimate children of God, none of us were unwanted or unexpected accidents. . . . We are not castoffs in an orphanage acting on our best behavior so someone might adopt us. Titus 3:4–5 tells us, "But when the kindness and love of God our Savior appeared, he saved us, not because of righteous things we had done, but because of his mercy."[7]

The apostle Paul described this concept a few thousand years ago in his letters to the Romans and to the Ephesians. "So you should not be like cowering, fearful slaves," he said. "You should behave instead like God's very own children, adopted into his family—calling him 'Father, dear Father.' For his Holy Spirit speaks to us deep in our hearts and tells us that we are God's children. And since we are his children, we will share his treasures—for everything God gives to his Son, Christ, is ours, too" (Rom. 8:15–17 NLT).

This is often a difficult concept for those of us who have lived through a divorce of our parents—even if our parents remarry and provide us stepparents to fill the gap. Anderson relates the story of two brothers that he met after a speaking engagement. The boys' mother and father had divorced, and later the mother remarried. Now grown, both men struggled with experiencing God's acceptance because they had never felt truly accepted and adopted by their stepfather. According to Anderson, the stepfather "wasn't a bad person, but the [sons] never connected with him. There was never a bonding relationship, not even with their mother. Consequently, their relationship with God was only theological, as their relationship with their parents was only functional."[8]

That's not the way God intended for you and me to relate to him! He has reached out toward each of us, offering more than mere acceptance. Instead, our heavenly Father has lavished his love on us, adopting us as his very own children.

The apostle Paul declares:

His unchanging plan has always been to adopt us into his own family by bringing us to himself through Jesus Christ. And this gave him great pleasure. . . . Furthermore, because of Christ, we have received an inheritance from God, for he chose us from the beginning, and all things happen just as he decided long ago.

Ephesians 1:5, 11 NLT

What wonderful news this is! Unfortunately, we often let the circumstances of our current life distract us from the benefits of God's adoptive acceptance. We forget that the primary responsibility of any adoptive parent is to lovingly care daily for the new child, to provide all the physical, emotional, mental, and spiritual nourishment that is within the parent's ability to give.

When we are accepted and adopted by God, there is no limit to God's loving care and ability to provide what we need! Sadly, though, we are often like the children in a nameless orphanage who cried themselves to sleep every night. Many of these kids had been abandoned in poverty, literally living on the streets, scavenging scraps of food out of garbage cans. Many a night these lost and lonely young ones had gone to sleep with only the sharp pangs of hunger to fill their empty stomachs. Many a night they fell asleep on a cold doorstep, wondering where they would find food the next day.

But then the children were rescued, taken to live in a warm home where they were cared for by adult volunteers who fed them, loved them, and provided warm, clean beds for them to sleep in. Each night they were fed until they were filled, then tucked into the safety of the orphanage dormitory.

Yet every night first one, then another, then most of them would begin sobbing in fear and sorrow. The volunteer parents did their best to comfort the distraught children but couldn't understand why they cried night after night.

Finally, one of the foster parents realized what was happening. The children worried themselves to tears, not because they were hungry or thirsty or cold but because they were scared that when they woke up they might have to go hungry once more. Nothing in their young lives to that point had given them any promise of tomorrow, and so they fretted themselves until the sobs came, scared that they might have nothing to eat when morning came.

The adults in the orphanage came up with a solution. Each night when the children were put to bed, each boy and girl was given a large bread roll that could be held or tucked under a pillow for safekeeping all night long. No matter when the child woke up—at midnight or early in the morning—that roll guaranteed at least one more day of food, giving the reassurance of at least one more day of security for the child.

Soon after, the sniffles and tears that had accompanied bedtime disappeared. Confident of the foster parents' provision for them, the children dropped quickly off to peaceful, confident sleep.[9]

Friend, sometimes it's easy for you and me to fret away the joy of God's acceptance, to remember our past losses and worry that God has somehow limited his adoption benefits toward us. If that's the case for you today, then let this book be your "nighttime roll" to remind you of this truth. God accepts you; he has chosen you; he has adopted you into his everlasting, glorious family. You are a treasured child of your limitless heavenly Father!

Your Father Accepts You Just as You Are

I'd like to tell you a true story about a woman I'll call Mary (not her real name). Mary lived in a small, rural town—you know the type, the kind of place where everybody knows everybody's business, and nobody's life is outside the scrutiny of others. For many in that town, this was a good arrangement. Their lives reflected high morals and status-enhancing activities.

For Mary this was not the case. No one knows for sure why she sought to fill her soul by filling her life with sexual indiscretions, but she did. Perhaps it was her low financial status; maybe she liked the gifts that men brought her in exchange for her sexual favors. Possibly she had been shunned by her own father, and that drove her into the arms of other men in desperate attempts to find love. Maybe she just wanted to feel accepted, to belong to someone and have that someone belong to her.

Whatever the reason, she shared her bed with a succession of men. She married five of them (each at a different time, of course), but each husband left her in the end, either through death or divorce. Finally, she took up residence with a sixth lover. This time she didn't bother to put on appearances by adding a wedding to the mix. Everyone knew the kind of woman she was anyway (or at least thought they did)—a slut, a tramp, barely more than a prostitute, really.

And so she lived a lonely existence—used by men for their pleasures, shunned by the women of the town as a low-class harlot not worthy of their friendship.

In Mary's little town there was a well where the village women gathered each day to collect water for their needs. Oh, but it was more than just a chore. The women gathered early in the mornings, laughing, chatting, and gossiping about anything and everything. It was a community time, where friends were made and sisterhood strengthened. Mary had tried going for water during these early morning gatherings. The disdainful looks and reproachful comments from the others had finally put an end to that. That was okay, though, Mary decided. She liked to sleep in anyway. So she made it her custom to venture out to the well in the afternoon, when the sun shone hot and the watering place was almost always deserted.

One day, though, when Mary went out to collect her pitcher of water, she found a man seated by the well, a foreigner, no less, a Jew, the people from whom Mary's mixed-blood ancestry hailed, but the people who also despised her kind for their lack of racial purity. In Mary's society, Jews, especially religious leaders—as this man seemed to be— simply didn't mix with her kind, with women of low reputation like she was.

Yet there he sat, staring at her with interest, not ogling her "assets" as so many other men had but truly noticing her, inviting her into his presence with some unspoken communication.

Finally, the words came. "Give me a drink," he said with a curious smile, motioning toward her pitcher and the well.

Something about the man made Mary feel flustered, but she managed to turn to him with a haughty air and retort, "How is it that you, a Jew, ask a drink of me, a woman of Samaria?"

The man's smile grew tender. "If you knew the gift of God and who it is that is saying to you, 'Give me a drink,' you would have asked him and he would have given you living water."

Mary felt a surge of adrenaline. Who was this strange man? And why did he act like he knew her, knew her better than she knew herself? She felt like running away, but something about him made her stay, made her carry on the conversation he had so unexpectedly started. And with each word he spoke, she grew more confused and clearheaded at the same time. They talked of life, of thirst, of eternity, and more.

Finally, he said, "Go, call your husband and come here."

She didn't respond at first, though the red flush in her face told her story all too well. After a moment she replied, "I have no husband."

There was that tender, knowing smile again. "You are right in saying 'I have no husband,' " he said calmly, "for you have had five husbands and the one you now have is not your husband."

Mary cringed, waiting for the harsh judgment that she felt sure would come. This man was obviously a prophet! He had known all along the sordid, trashy affairs of her miserable existence. He had been toying with her, like a cat plays with a mouse before devouring its prey. So she waited, preparing for the torrent of hate and rejection that was sure to come.

But there was only silence. Mary dared a glimpse into the stranger's eyes. What she saw there shocked her. He knew her, knew her evil ways and disappointing past, yet he did not let it soil the look in his eyes. In them, instead of judgment, was acceptance, compassion, love.

In moments she knew. This was no ordinary man. It was the Messiah, the promised One come to save people from their sins. Mary had come face-to-face with Jesus Christ himself—and he had welcomed her into his presence, into his life.

Joy began to well up within her, threatening to burst forth out of her belly. The acceptance of the Savior had brought renewal of the heart, revival of the soul. As a result, she became the first missionary/evangelist in the land of Samaria. She literally ran with excitement back into her village and proclaimed, "Come, see a man who told me all I ever did. Can this be the Christ?" And the Bible records that, as a result of her personal testimony, many in that village put their faith in Jesus Christ![10]

Just as he did to that scorned, outcast woman of Samaria, Jesus holds his arms of love and acceptance toward you and me, right at this moment, just as we are. And just like that woman, when we enter into his spiritual embrace, he transforms us, from the inside out, until we too can't help but bring others to him by sharing about the life-changing power of even one encounter with God!

Your Father's Acceptance Empowers You to Accept Others

Let me repeat a few things. God is your Father, and he is always ready to welcome you into his presence. Better yet, he not only offers you unconditional acceptance, he extends to you adoption and makes you a fully endowed member of his eternal family. What's more, though your Father accepts you just as you are, his presence in your life cannot help but transform you into something better than you really are— an image of Jesus Christ himself.

Let me tell you one last truth about this subject before I close this chapter. You see, your Father's acceptance of you does one thing more. It empowers you to become one who can accept others as an expression of his unconditional love. This power of acceptance is truly supernatural, and it breaches all boundaries of race and color and religious background and societal status and country of origin and more. The fact that God has accepted and adopted you can enable you to accept the fact that your parents are not perfect—and to love them anyway. It enables you to go beyond your comfort zone to reach out to those who are your friends, your coworkers, and, yes, even your enemies.

I think one of the most beautiful examples of this truth was found in the life and work of Mother Teresa of Calcutta. For decades she lived in the slums of India, scouring the streets for the "poorest of the poor," providing hope, love, and a clean, warm place to die in peace.

I read a short biography of this woman's life, and one event has stayed with me long after the reading.[11] It was 1955, and together with several of her companion nuns, Teresa had finally opened the place that was her dream, a shelter called Nirmal Hriday, which means Place of the Pure Heart. This place has only one real function—to be a home for the dying, a place where the terminally ill can go to die in peace.

Nirmal Hriday was located right next door to a Hindu temple, and the workers at that temple were fuming about the fact that Mother Teresa's Christian faith would be expressed so near to their bastion of Hinduism. They were outraged that others might see her example and turn from Hinduism to Christianity.

Daily these religious people gathered outside Nirmal Hriday, shouting curses, demanding that Mother Teresa and her workers leave, threatening to kill the nuns, and occasionally even throwing stones at the women who ran the shelter. And daily the nuns ignored the protests (and ducked when the stones flew by), continuing their work.

Then one day Mother Teresa noticed a large crowd had gathered on the sidewalk outside the doors of Nirmal Hriday. Curious, she went out and discovered the people circled around a man who was dying and covered in his own vomit. The man was suffering from cholera, a highly contagious—and deadly—disease. No one would touch the man for fear of catching his disease and suffering a similar fate, and so he was left a reject, left alone in a crowd of people.

On closer inspection, Mother Teresa saw that this wretched man was her enemy—well, one of them at least. He was a Hindu priest, one of the many that had opposed her work next door to his temple. Some might even say he was now getting what he deserved, suffering humility and pain for his despicable treatment of the nuns.

Without hesitation Mother Teresa waded into the crowd and knelt by the dirty man's side. Lifting him herself, she carried him from the street to the inside of Nirmal Hriday. There she lovingly washed the filth from his body and placed him in a clean bed, away from the gawking eyes of his so-called Hindu friends. Then she sat with him, tending him for the next few hours until his ravaged body finally succumbed to the illness. He died, but thanks to the unconditional acceptance of a little Christian woman, he at least was allowed to die in peace and dignity.

The Hindus stopped attacking Mother Teresa and her nuns. They had seen the unconditional love of God, expressed in this woman's ability to accept someone they themselves could not.

Friend, that is the power of your Father's acceptance in you. That is the strength that comes from being adopted into the family of God. Have I realized that power fully yet? No, and perhaps you haven't either. But it doesn't matter.

What does matter is that God's loving adoption of us has the unfathomable ability both to overcome the pain and rejection we felt as children of divorce and to empower us to sweep away the bitterness that rejection has caused in other people's lives. This is the power that lies within your grasp—God's unconditional acceptance, held out to you daily on the fingertips of your heavenly Father.

Something to Think About . . .

Use the following questions either by yourself or with a group to process what you've learned in this chapter.

- Who is the person in your life who best demonstrates unconditional acceptance toward you? How does that person reflect the way God feels about you?
- What's the difference between "acceptance" and "adoption"? What does it mean to you today—right now— that God chooses to adopt you into his eternal family?
- When have you seen, or experienced, the transforming power of your heavenly Father's acceptance?
- How can God's unconditional acceptance of you today help you demonstrate acceptance toward others tomorrow?

Something to Do

Adopt a pet! If you can afford it (and your household will allow it), visit a local animal shelter and take home a dog or a cat. If that's just not practical for your life situation right now, visit a discount store (like Wal Mart or Target) and pick up a small plush animal instead.

Give your new pet a name like Orphan or Annie or Oliver Twist or Adoption Dog (or something better!), and let that pet be a constant reminder to you that God has chosen to accept and adopt you into his eternal family.

5

A Father Who Disciplines You

Not long ago, the sheriff's office in an anonymous town in Texas published some advice for parents. They called it, "How to Raise a Juvenile Delinquent in Your Own Family."[1] Curious as to what it said? It went like this:

1. Begin with infancy to give the child everything he wants. This will insure his believing that the world owes him a living.
2. Pick up everything he leaves lying around. This will teach him he can always throw off responsibility on others.
3. Take his part against neighbors, teachers, policemen. They are all prejudiced against your child. He is a "free spirit" and never wrong.

4. Finally, prepare yourself for a life of grief. You're going to have it.

What a perfect reminder of the value of discipline in a child's life! Unfortunately, discipline is also one of the major areas in which a divorced parent is most likely to overreact in regard to his or her children. As a result, you and I have likely entered adulthood with a warped view of God's discipline in our lives.

Popular author and speaker Josh McDowell identifies four primary parenting styles in regard to discipline.[2] The ideal style, he asserts, is what he calls the "relational" model. That is discipline within the context of an intimate relationship between a parent and a child, one that offers support and love while also setting reasonable, defined limits on behavior and expectations. The relational style of child discipline works because it balances—and communicates— the parent's love and the parent's desire to help the child grow into a healthy, capable, self-sustaining individual.

I've got to tell you, that's not the kind of discipline I received as a child, despite my mother's good intentions. You see, the complicated pressures and circumstances of post-divorce life conspired against my whole family, interfering with everything—especially a boy's need for daily, relationship-focused discipline. Financial pressures often made it necessary for my mother to work two or three jobs to support our family, meaning there were often days when we barely saw each other. Educational concerns also took time away, as she pursued (and earned) a doctorate at the same time. Social obligations, school grades and activities, even church membership responsibilities, all taken together, meant that I grew up with an absent father and, out of necessity, an often-inaccessible mother.

The result was that, at my home, the parental discipline ricocheted like a pinball between the other three styles McDowell describes: autocratic, permissive, and neglectful. I'm guessing you experienced something like this too.

On her "autocratic" days (which usually occurred when I got in trouble at school or in a fight with my sisters), my mother would put her foot down and shout the equivalent of "It's my way or the highway!" When this happened, she and I either had a knock-down-drag-out argument, or I'd appease her with empty promises and sneak out after she'd gone to sleep to do whatever it was I wanted to do anyway.

When she was just too exhausted to do more than lie on the couch and recover, she'd adopt the permissive style. "Do what you want," she'd say then. "I trust you." While I liked the freedom of this style, I was woefully immature for that kind of responsibility.

And, sadly, the neglectful style of discipline showed up all too often in my home. My mother was busy, stressed out, overworked yet deeply in debt, and had her hands full with my older siblings as well. That meant that from the time I was eleven, I was pretty much on my own. When I got in trouble, it was up to me to figure a way out of it. When I needed to accomplish a big homework assignment, it was up to me to schedule out my time to get it done (which created a habit of procrastination that haunted many of my nights even into college).

In short, for many years I viewed discipline as an intermittent, irrelevant thing. Imagine my surprise when I discovered that my heavenly Father thought otherwise! I found that he not only practices discipline with his children—he intends it for me too. And sometimes (okay, nearly all the time) I was none too happy to receive it.

Then (it took too long, I admit it) I finally realized that my Father's discipline was not an act meant to punish me or make me suffer out of retaliation for my constant sinfulness. When he took out the figurative "heavenly belt" to give me a spiritual whipping, his motivation was not anger but love. Since that's such an important truth, let's spend a little time with it now.

Your Father's Discipline Is an Act of Love

Gen. H. Norman Schwarzkopf is best known for his strategic, winning leadership during the Gulf War. The good general also served in Vietnam as a colonel in command of the First Battalion of the Sixth Infantry of the U.S. Army.

For a time his troops were stationed on the Batangan Peninsula, an area that had been the focus of battles for three decades and that was covered with hidden land mines and explosives. Mindful of the dangers, Schwarzkopf instituted strict procedures to reduce the risk of casualties, and whenever a soldier was injured, the commander himself flew out in his personal helicopter to evacuate the American and take him back to safety and medical care.

On May 28, 1970, despite all their efforts, a soldier stepped on a land mine that exploded and critically injured him. Norman immediately flew out to help in the evacuation. While he was there, another soldier, who was helping in the rescue attempt, also stepped on a mine. The resulting explosion threatened to take the man's leg off and left him screaming and writhing in pain on the ground.

At that moment it suddenly dawned on Schwarzkopf and his fellow soldiers that they weren't dealing with a single mine left behind as a remnant of war. They were actually standing in the middle of a minefield, with untold numbers of other bombs hidden all around them, waiting to go off at the slightest pressure from another soldier's boot. In fact the more that the injured soldier rolled and wailed on the ground, the more likely he was to set off another, possibly deadly, explosion! I'll let General Schwarzkopf describe what happened next:

"I started through the minefield, one slow step at a time, staring at the ground, looking for telltale bumps or little prongs sticking up from the dirt. My knees were shaking so hard that each time I took a step, I had to grab my leg and

71

steady it with both hands before I could take another. . . . It seemed like a thousand years before I reached the kid."

Notice what Schwarzkopf did when he finally arrived at the injured man. He didn't pause to gently rebuke the soldier for thrashing around and endangering himself even more. He didn't tap him on the shoulder, hoping to get his attention, and then reason with him about the dangers of rolling uncontrollably in the middle of a minefield. He didn't extol the virtues of discipline when surrounded by enemy mines and explain long and hard about how the soldier's current lack of discipline could realistically get him killed.

Instead, the 240-pound hero pounced on the injured man, using brute strength to overpower and pin him to the ground. Only after he had imposed his lifesaving discipline on the wounded fighter did he begin to explain the situation, calming the man down until he understood and was able to control himself once more.[3]

If Norman Schwarzkopf had refused to discipline his wounded soldier, that would not have shown any love for the man in his care. In fact we would all agree that would have been callous, irresponsible neglect—possibly even hatred—for that man. The greatest love the general showed that day was in his willingness to tackle and pin his injured comrade—to instill physical discipline and save his life in the process.

Imagine, now, applying our typical expectations of God to this scenario. *God, I'm hurting here! Life has injured me! I'm in great pain! Now, wait a second, though. Don't you dare try to touch me. You'll just make it hurt worse. Hey, what are you doing? Get off me! Ouch! You're killing me! Stop limiting my ability to move! Can't you see you're lying right on my injured leg? Are you blind? Or deaf? Or do you just hate me so much you want to cause me more suffering than I've already got? I knew it! I knew it all along! You don't love me; you never did! All you want to do is pin me to the ground so I will writhe in painful, helpless agony! Oh, woe is me!*

It's a ridiculous picture, isn't it? Yet, sadly, that's the way we often view the disciplining hand of God in our lives. He who is our greatest Friend, who has weighed our current actions with their future consequences and chosen to intercede on our behalf, it is he whom we call our enemy.

"God's out to get me! Why else would he let me get fired from my job?"

"God has forgotten me. Why else would he allow me to suffer this chronic illness?"

"God's greatest pleasure is to make my life difficult. Why else would he allow my family to be such an emotionally trying group of people?"

We just don't get it. When God chooses to discipline us, our Father has one—and only one—motivation—love. It is God's love for us that will not allow him to sit idly by while we, his children, insanely pursue attitudes and actions that will cause us harm. Like the parent who displays relational discipline, God reaches out one hand to support us and with the other administers a sometimes painful (okay, often painful) correcting influence to bring us out of the spiral of sin and into the healthy habits of Jesus Christ, his Son.

Do you see what that means? When we feel the sting of God's rebuke, he is not treating us as strangers or enemies. It is in those moments, though we are loath to admit it, that God is reminding us that we are *his kids,* his beloved children who deserve better than what we've given ourselves.

Here is how theologian Harold Willmington explains it: "It's true! He does it because he loves us. . . . God's discipline of a sinning Christian does not imply condemnation but rather confirmation, *demonstrating that we belong to him.*"[4]

Perhaps now is a good time for us to remember the words of the apostle Paul in Hebrews 12:5–11 (NLT; italics mine):

> And have you entirely forgotten the encouraging words God spoke to you, his children? He said,
>
> > "My child, don't ignore it when the Lord disciplines you, and don't be discouraged when he corrects you. For the Lord disciplines those he loves, and he punishes those he accepts as his children."
>
> As you endure this divine discipline, *remember that God is treating you as his own children.* Whoever heard of a child who was never disciplined? If God doesn't discipline you as he does all of his children, it means that you are illegitimate and are not really his children after all. . . . No discipline is enjoyable while it is happening—it is painful! But afterward there will be a quiet harvest of right living for those who are trained in this way.

Remember what I told you back in chapter 2 of this book? Your Father loves you. Now, if that is true (which it is), then we must also be willing to recognize the fact that because God loves us, he will discipline us. Our Father won't leave us flopping in dangerous, uncontrolled agony in the middle of the minefield of life. He will always come to us, always endure with us, and, when necessary, use his mighty frame to pin us to the ground in discipline, teaching us to follow his way to safety and health.

As Josh McDowell says:

> God is good. He is a loving Father. He is a perfect Father. His intentions and His actions are never evil or unloving. Yet He disciplines His children. He does not discipline in spite of His goodness, He disciplines because of His goodness. He

74

does not discipline in spite of His love, He disciplines because of His love.[5]

Your Father Uses Many Tools to Bring Out the Best in You

The knowledge that God's discipline is an act of love doesn't mean there are no more questions about this topic, however. For instance, how do we, God's children, recognize our Father's discipline in our lives? We know that not everything bad that happens is God's disciplining hand in our lives, but how do we know which is which?

I wish I could tell you that I know the definitive answers to these questions, but I don't! All I can do at this point is share with you a few truths I know about God and offer a few observations I've learned over the past two decades in which I've been a Christian.

First, I know that there is no limit to God's power, to his love for you, or to his creativity in dealing with people. One look at a giraffe or a puppy or even at your remarkable face should be proof enough of that! Can you make a giraffe or care enough about people to invent a puppy for a companion or spend eternity lovingly etching every line, every pore on every face? God can use anything and everything in any and every way at any and every time to accomplish his purpose in your life. (For more on this, see Matt. 19:26; Jer. 32:17; Job 42:2; Gen. 1:1.)

Second, the end result of your Father's discipline in your life is to help you become more like his only perfect Son, Jesus Christ. It is a process that is preparing you for more than just this life, but for eternity with him. (For more on this, see Eph. 2:10; 4:24; Phil. 2:1–5; 1 Cor. 15:49.)

So how does God discipline us in this life? I've learned a few ways, and though I know this list isn't exhaustive, let me share with you what I've experienced.

Time-Out/Denial of Privileges

Like a preschooler sent to sit in a corner during recess, I've often endured being placed on "time-out" from God. There are times (too often, I must admit) when I become so enamored with myself and so intent on doing what I want to do, that God must occasionally "blow the whistle" and set me aside for a time. And like that preschooler, I will sit there until I gain a better understanding of what is appropriate behavior—which, in my case, usually means turning my focus off myself and back on my Father.

Sometimes God will use physical ailments to bring this kind of time-out for me. I suffer from a chronic stomach ailment that causes me to feel some level of nausea most every day. Fortunately, this condition, while not curable, is treatable with medicine that allows me to function almost normally. There are times, however, when it's all I can do simply to get out of bed for an entire day. It is as if God has seen me taking my health for granted and given me a short denial of the privilege of good health (much like a parent might take away the privilege of driving a car for a week).

I've found that, much as I dislike those "slow days" as we call them, God often uses them as brief "time-outs" for me where I am physically forced to stop whatever I'm doing or planning to do and instead refocus my attention and attitudes on God.

Sometimes God will use mental frustration ("writer's block") to make me take a time-out. For instance, a few weeks ago, I had scheduled myself to work on a chapter of this book. Each day I sat down, it was almost as if a curtain had been pulled across my mind; no matter what I tried, I simply could *not* find the words to put on the page. After about four days of this, I finally got the message. I put aside the book for a while and spent time praying about it instead. When I finally picked it up again, the chapter flowed as if a spigot had been unstopped, and I finished it in record time.

In that instance, I truly believe God was gently correcting me, reminding me that all my words mean nothing unless he has been involved in the creative process.

Other time-outs I've experienced (and I'm sure you have too) have been the loss of a job, working in a job that had little meaning for me, being left out of leadership opportunities, and more. The important thing to remember during those time-outs is not just how long they last but how quickly you allow them to refocus your heart, mind, soul, and body on the face of your heavenly Father.

The Dreaded Lecture

My twelve-year-old son says the worst "punishment" I give him is a lecture. It is, of course, those times when I sit him down and explain in exquisite detail why it is wrong to do things like practice his football tackling technique on creaky ol' Dad when Dad isn't looking, or when I deliver all the scientific evidence supporting a regular bedtime for adolescents.

I've found that often God seems to give me this "dreaded lecture" treatment. Though I will invariably roll my eyes or try to explain to God just why my way is better than his, I've also discovered that if I actually listen during these times when God is speaking, it saves me great heartache and troubles later! When do I hear these lectures from God? Most often during my times of reading the Bible, when the words of God penetrate my heart and convict me of the sin that is so obvious in my life. Other times, I hear God's corrective voice in a sermon my pastor delivers or in a song from a Christian artist I admire or in the gentle rebuke of my wife, friends, and family.

Truthfully, this disciplinary method of God shows itself all over my life. Only my stubborn, stiff-necked pride keeps me from hearing—and learning—from God's voice each day.

Natural Consequences

When I ignore God's voice in my life, I tend to experience the next step in God's corrective process—the consequences of my actions. Those short-tempered words I speak to my wife result in an unnecessary argument over whether or not the dining room table can hold both dishes and a week's worth of mail. My impatience at the driver in front of me in traffic results in a police officer ticketing me for tailgating. My lack of discipline regarding regular exercise means I'm short of breath after running around the backyard with my son for just a few moments.

Of course, God allows more severe discipline to come as a natural consequence too, for instance, the smoker who eventually develops lung cancer or the drinker who ends up in a car wreck while driving under the influence of alcohol. Funny thing about this form of discipline from God, though. I've found it's almost always avoidable—especially if we take the time to listen when he's giving the "dreaded lecture."

Spanking

Despite all efforts otherwise, God sometimes must use extreme measures to regain the attention of his children. When this happens, I call it a "spanking" from God. Televangelist Jim Bakker experienced this, I think. After years of greed and deceit and moments of lust that consummated in sexual adultery, God finally brought devastating punishment. Bakker's sins brought him public humiliation, financial ruin, and even a prison sentence. Yet, afterward, that disciplining action of God brought Bakker back to his Father and even resulted in an apologetic biography, which the man contritely titled *I Was Wrong*.[6]

"What is God trying to do when He allows His children to go through hard trials and deep suffering?" asks Ray Pritchard in his excellent little book *FAQ*.

There are several answers to that question. First, God is purging us of sin and purifying us of iniquity. Second, God uses suffering to test our faith. . . . Third, God uses difficulty to humble us. When things are going well, we tend to get puffed up about our accomplishments. But let the darkness fall and we are on our knees crying out to God.[7]

I've heard it said that God will do whatever it takes to bring his children back home—even if it means allowing them to suffer so greatly that their only recourse is to fall on the mercy of God. Friend, this is not what any of us would desire, but like General Schwarzkopf's harsh treatment of the wounded soldier, it is sometimes everything we need. Thank God that he is willing to let us suffer so that we may be saved! (But if we are wise, we will heed his discipline long before it must come to this!)

Your Father's Discipline Is Always Right

I heard once of an army officer who had a unique method of disciplining soldiers in his command who had quarreled with each other. If tempers flared and one man lashed out at another in anger, the orders were clear, and the commanding officer followed them.

The two disgruntled soldiers were ordered to wash the same window—one on the outside, one on the inside. They were to clean it to a shining brilliance, knowing it would be inspected afterward.

Ludwig Bemelmans, an army officer who used this method, reports on the results of this unusual disciplinary action. "Looking at each other, they soon have to laugh and all is forgotten. It works; I have tried it."[8]

Why do I tell you this little story at this point? Because I want to remind you of something important about God's discipline. Like two soldiers ordered to wash a window inside and out, we may not always understand the disciplinary tactic that God uses to bring us in line with his will—and that's okay. We don't have to understand the way God works; we simply have to trust that if we cooperate with his way of correcting us, our Father will use it to bring about what is right in our lives.

Unfortunately, that's often easier said than done! Too often we are like the child who was sent to bed without supper for misbehaving. Five minutes later, the boy called out to his father. "Dad," he said, "I'm thi-i-i-irsty! Would you bring me a glass of water?"

The father was firm. "No, son. You knew what would happen if you disobeyed. Now go to sleep."

After a few minutes of silence, the boy called out again. "Dad, I'm still thirsty! Can I please have a drink of water now?"

"No," the father replied. "And if you ask again, I'm going to have to spank you."

Five more minutes passed, then the boy called out one last time. "Da-ad! When you come in to spank me, would you bring me a glass of water?"[9]

We chuckle at this little boy's persistence, but the truth is, if he had chosen not to misbehave, he would never have had to endure a spanking or thirst that fateful night! It's sad that we are also often shortsighted when it comes to our Father's correction in our lives. We, through our own attitudes and actions, necessitate a disciplinary act from God. Then, instead of allowing the discipline to help mold us into the image of Christ, we stubbornly cry out to God for whatever it is we think we so desperately need—even to the point of welcoming harm to get it!

Here's a secret for you. You don't have to be like that. Next time you find yourself in a situation that could very well be God working correction in your life—such as a job loss, a financial crunch, a business trip with a person who annoys you, whatever—don't beg God for a way out. Rather, ask

God to help you complete the discipline so that you can grow more like him, moment by moment, day by day. If you do this, it will revolutionize the way you live.

"Discipline," says Dr. Peter Hirsch, "comes from the word 'disciple,' which means two very interesting things: *to follow* and *learner.* . . . Discipline comes from following and learning from someone or something."[10]

Theologian Wendell Johnston expands on this for us. He says:

> The concept of teaching and training—which includes attaining wisdom and doing what is right and proper—comes from the meaning of the words [for discipline] used in both Old and New Testaments. . . . The predominant emphasis in both Testaments is toward positive growth and development. . . . Punishment is never seen as an end in itself. Rather it is to bring out the best in an individual and ultimately cause him or her to glorify God.[11]

When we submit to the discipline of God—no matter how unorthodox it may seem—we actually bring ourselves into the role of disciple of God; we become children who are more than relatives of the Creator. We become children whose Father is also our greatest hero; we are kids who want to be just like their Daddy.

Your Father's Discipline Is Empowerment

As we move toward the end of this discussion of our Father's disciplining love for us, I think we need to deal with one last misconception about this topic.

"Sure, I want to be like Jesus," we sometimes say, "but God is so limiting! After all, isn't Christianity just a list of dos and don'ts? If I give in fully to God's discipline, that means I can't do all those things I like to do, all those things everybody else is free to do whenever they want. I'll be like a bird trapped in a cage!"

With all due respect, that kind of attitude is a big load of hooey, no matter how many times you hear people spout it off to you. Here are Elisabeth Elliot's comments on this subject:

> Freedom and discipline have come to be regarded as mutually exclusive, when in fact freedom is not at all the opposite, but the final reward, of discipline. It is to be bought with a high price, not merely claimed. . . . The [professional] skater and [race] horse are free to perform as they do only because they have been subjected to countless hours of grueling work, rigidly prescribed, faithfully carried out. Men are free to soar into space because they have willingly confined themselves in a tiny capsule designed and produced by highly trained scientists and craftsmen, have meticulously followed instructions and submitted themselves to rules which others defined.[12]

Recently my basketball-loving son and I watched the classic Gene Hackman movie *Hoosiers*.[13] In this film, based on a true story, Hackman plays Norman Dale, a newly hired coach at a little high school in rural Indiana. Coach Dale has his work cut out for him, with not the least of his problems being he's got only six students who try out for his team! Despite that, he is determined to mold these young men of Hickory High School into a championship caliber team.

The first thing he discovers is that his students are decent players—but in no way a team. They play as individuals and resist his efforts to blend them together. Finally, the time comes for the Hickory Huskers to take the court in their first game of the season.

"Okay, guys," Coach Dale reminds his team before the tip-off, "a minimum of four passes before you take a shot."

The boys hit the court, and at first they try to follow their coach's instructions. But they are getting hammered and by halftime are well behind in the score. Finally, one of the star players, Rade Butcher (played by Steve Hollar), has had enough. On his team's first possession to start the second half, he dribbles the ball down the court and without a glance at his teammates puts up a twenty footer. It swishes through the basket as the crowd cheers in approval.

Ignoring his coach completely now, he does it again the next time he gets the ball. The spectators are beside themselves with excitement, yelling out, "Good job, Rade!" and chanting, "Let's go, Rade!"

But the coach, sitting on the sidelines, realizes what will happen if he refuses to discipline Rade, in spite of his success. As each game progresses during the season, his team will become more and more fragmented. They will play with a selfishness that will soon eliminate them from any possibility of winning more than a handful of games against obviously weaker opponents.

So he does what he must do. To the outrage of the fans, he orders Rade to come out of the game and sit on the bench while an obviously inferior player takes his place on the court.

Moments later, another player fouls out of the game. Since there are only six players total on the team, and five are expected to be on the court at all times, most fans assume that means Rade will be allowed back onto the court.

Without even looking at his coach, Rade Butcher jumps up and prepares to enter the game.

"Where you going?" says Coach Dale.

"In the game," Rade responds.

"Sit down," the coach commands.

"What do you mean?" Rade protests. "We gotta have five out there."

"Sit down," the coach orders again. "Sit!"

Rade reluctantly returns to the bench. Moments later, the referee runs over and advises, "Coach, you need one more."

And Coach Dale just points to the court and says with determination, "My team is on the floor."

He has made his choice. He knows that discipline now will be difficult for Rade and the others to take. But he also knows that if they learn the teamwork discipline now, they will all be better players in the end.

So the Hickory High School Huskers finish out their game with only four players on the court! They lose, of course, but the lesson they learn about team play is one they will always remember.

Coach Norman Dale was willing to make his team endure embarrassment and defeat so that they would learn—and take to heart—this fundamental concept of discipline. By limiting his players and forcing them into losing this game, he gave them knowledge and a team desire that empowered them to win the state championship later that season.

God's discipline is like that. Our Father knows the opponents we are up against—enemies like a sin nature, selfishness, and the devil himself. But he also knows what it will take for us to triumph over those opponents, and his discipline will do whatever it takes to empower us to become champions in the end.

Will God allow us to be embarrassed? Yes, because it means we will be exalted with him in eternity.

Will our Father allow us to get whipped by the enemy from time to time? Yes, because he knows that those whippings will build in us a strength and resolve that will send Satan crying home to hell when the time comes.

Will he let our mistakes bring pain and sorrow to those we love? Yes, because by doing that, we will learn the terrible consequences of our sin.

You see, when we learn not to fight God's discipline, when we embrace it instead, it frees us to become all that we were intended to be. It empowers us to be champions like nothing else we try ever will or ever could. Submission to God's disciplining force in our lives enables us to become like the athlete who daily endures the rigors and heartaches (and body aches) of training so that he or she will one day stand at the finish line with the winning medal held high.

Is this an easy path to take? Of course not. But it is the only path to greatness, and as such it's the one that God our Father is determined to see us take. So, remember, God's discipline in your life isn't intended simply to limit your "freedom"; it's designed to empower you with the freedom to succeed beyond your greatest expectations.

As I close this chapter, I want to leave you with one final word of advice on this topic of the discipline needed to succeed in life. It's a quote from Al Rosen of the Cleveland Indians:

> The most complete athletes are those who strive to overcome their weaknesses by hard work and persistence. Practicing on one's strengths is more enjoyable and obviously much easier, but working long and hard on one's weaknesses, while it may be the more difficult path to follow, has the certain assurance of success.[14]

Your parents' divorce started you off in life as an underdog. Now your Father stands ready to coach you, ready to teach you to overcome your weaknesses by hard work, persistence, and a strong reliance on his Holy Spirit's power and discipline. Sure, it will be difficult at times, but if you heed his training, you are guaranteed to win. Now you and I must ask ourselves, why would we ever want to do anything else but that?

Something to Think About . . .

Use the following questions either by yourself or with a group to process what you've learned in this chapter.

- What makes us naturally resistant to the discipline of God?
- How does it make you feel to understand that God's motivation for disciplining you is not anger or revenge but is, instead, love? Explain your answer.
- How can you increase your ability to trust God's discipline when it just doesn't make any sense to you?
- In what ways has God's discipline empowered you to succeed in the past? How can it help you succeed in the future?

Something to Do

Rent and enjoy the movie *Hoosiers*. As you watch it, see if you can identify any parallels between Coach Dale's discipline and the way God disciplines each one of us, his children.

6

A Father Who
Forgives You

I have to admit, I have a few bad habits. I seem to have cultivated them over the course of my life. For starters, I sometimes leave the toilet seat up. Also, I can't stand for anyone else to hold the remote control when I'm in the room. And I even chew my fingernails.

No worries, though, because my wife has a few bad habits of her own. She can't seem to close a cabinet door to save her life. And she chews her ice, making loud crunching noises that drive her sister crazy.

Lest my wife and I feel too bad about ourselves, there are also many others with terrible habits. It's common knowledge that smoking tobacco can cause life-threatening diseases, yet millions of Americans smoke anyway. Alcohol consumption results in thousands of deaths and injuries each year, but millions of folks still drink too much. Obesity can also be deadly, yet millions of us live on fatty, fast-food diets anyway.

Let's face it; we've all got bad habits, some more dangerous than others. But right now I want us to focus on two habits in particular, because these two are ones that we children of divorce often cultivate in our lives—yet are reluctant to talk about. What are those two bad habits of ours? False strength and hidden weakness.

You see, when our parents divorced, we were told to "grow up" and to "be strong." From my preschool days, I remember family and relatives telling me, "You're the man of the house, now, Mikey. You have to be strong for all of us."

So I learned to put on a mask of bravado, to stay calm when everything seemed to be going crazy. I dried my tears and rarely let them flow in public, no matter what. I was the man of the house, after all. I learned a cold self-reliance that practically shouted, "I don't need a father; I don't need you; I don't need anybody. I can do whatever I need to do all by myself."

False strength.

And down below the surface was what I refused to admit to others—hidden weakness. Sin that runs through my blood poisoned me from the inside out, affecting everything I did, every relationship I ever entered, every task I strove to perform, tainting every attitude and motive with selfishness.

You know what I'm talking about, don't you? You've been there. You've seen the admiring looks of people who whispered, "He's handling the divorce very well for someone his age" or "She's grown into such a confident, capable woman, in spite of the hardships of her past." And you knew that even though others sometimes didn't see it, you'd failed, you'd kept a secret sin, you'd harbored a harmful habit.

False strength and hidden weakness are two bad habits that not only weaken our daily lives but hinder our relationship with our heavenly Father. See, he knows the truth. He isn't faked out by our brash words or secret sins.

Left to our own devices, we would be nothing but lost and condemned.

(Here comes the good news . . .) But our Father refused to leave us to our own bad habits. He has opened his arms in our direction, allowed Jesus to pay the penalty for our wrongdoings, and extended to us his limitless, relentless forgiveness.

Each day we can approach anew a Father who stands ready—and able—to forgive any offense, great or small!

Your Father's Forgiveness Is Freeing

As we begin the discussion of God's awesome forgiveness, I want to start by reminding you of this incredible truth. Your Father offers his forgiveness to you for free.

Unfortunately, we humans aren't often so honorably charitable. In fact, during the last days of Bill Clinton's presidency, it appears that forgiveness was up for sale. Although President Clinton denied any wrongdoing, the case of the pardon of Marc Rich in particular caused something of an uproar from Democrats and Republicans alike.[1]

At the time he was pardoned, Rich was ranked as the number six most wanted fugitive on the Department of Justice's list of international fugitives. He was also a multimillionaire living in luxury in Switzerland, with homes elsewhere, including a ten-million-dollar mansion on the coast of Spain.

After alleged shady dealings with terrorists and rogue nations, such as Libya, Iran, and Cuba, Rich was finally indicted on fifty-one counts of tax fraud in what one prosecutor called "the largest tax fraud in the history of the United States." Instead of facing the charges, Rich fled the country, renounced his U.S. citizenship, and set himself up overseas.

As the year 2000 approached, Marc Rich, his ex-wife Denise, and several cronies allegedly set in motion a scheme to convince President Clinton to grant him a full presidential pardon. Basically it boiled down to Denise Rich funneling money to the president and his causes and hoping that it would be enough to "buy" a pardon.

Denise Rich did her job well. She gave $450,000 to the Clinton Library foundation. She gave $100,000 to the Democratic National Committee, donated $109,000 to the Senate campaign of Hillary Rodham Clinton, and paid $40,000 for entertainment at Hillary Clinton's birthday party. She even gave $7,000 in furniture to Bill and Hillary Clinton and presented the president with a gift of a saxophone made of gold. In all, Barbara Olson, in her book *The Final Days,* reported, "Denise Rich gave $1.5 million to causes related to the Clintons."

Apparently that was enough. Just before he left office in January of 2001, President Bill Clinton pardoned Marc Rich and, by all outward appearances, sold the forgiveness of the U.S. government to a fugitive from justice.

God's forgiveness is the exact opposite of Bill Clinton's presidential pardon. There is no amount of money that can ever earn his grace, no flashy gift that can influence his divine favor. There is no price tag attached to your Father's forgiveness. He gives it freely, daily, hourly. In fact, would Marc Rich desire it, your Father would lavish that same grace on him that God offers to all of us.

Do you understand this great thing? Has it sunk in yet? Let me spell it out plainly one more time: *Your Father's forgiveness is free.*

When it comes to your failings, your "bad habits," your sins and crimes against God, his grace rules supreme. Thanks to the power of Jesus' vicarious death and resurrection, the price has been paid for you. One Christian dictionary defines what I'm talking about this way: "Grace: Unmerited and free favor and mercy shown to sinners by a sovereign God with a view to their salvation."[2]

But God's grace and forgiveness do not simply end there. Not only is your Father's mercy toward you free, it is *freeing*. It releases you from the penalty of sin that would reign over your life. Theologian Millard Erickson sheds light on the concept with this definition: "Forgiveness of sins: Pardon of wrongdoing. Forgiveness entails cancellation of any penalty sin may have incurred *and* of any ill feeling it may have aroused."[3]

Here is how another theologian, Lawrence Richards, expands on this truth: "Divine forgiveness does not overlook sin or dismiss it lightly," he says. "Rather, forgiveness is an act of God by which He deals, not with our guilt but with the sins themselves. In forgiveness, God removes the sins and makes the guilt moot."[4]

I heard a story once of a judge who one day saw an old, dear friend brought up before his bench for a crime. The case was tried and the judge's friend was declared guilty. Now it was time for sentencing, and everyone wondered if the judge would "go light" on the convicted criminal out of sentiment for their long friendship.

To the surprise of many in the courtroom, the judge issued the standard penalty—fourteen days of hard labor or a five-hundred-dollar fine. The convict had no money to speak of, and in sorrow, prepared himself for the cold, hard labor of prison.

But before the prisoner could be taken away, the judge stepped down from his bench, threw off his judge's robes, and stood next to the friend. In a moment, he had paid the friend's fine, thereby setting him free. "Now, John," the judge said warmly, "you are coming home with me to supper."[5]

That's what God's forgiveness in your life is like! It is finding out that the Judge is your Friend. Yes, you've done wrong; yes, you deserve punishment, but your Father has made the payment of your penalty, has set you free from the shackles of your own prison, and invited you to come home with him instead. *Your Father's forgiveness is freeing.*

Your Father's Forgiveness Enables You to Forgive Yourself

There are several aspects to the freeing power of God's grace in your life, but now I want to focus on one important fact. Your Father's forgiveness enables you to forgive yourself.

Here is an unusual aftereffect of divorce. Often the child of divorced parents harbors a secret guilt about the breakup. Though obviously not responsible for the parents' separation, the child still knows that he or she has not been perfect. Deep down, he or she wonders, *If only I'd been a better student . . . If only I'd been more obedient . . . If only I'd done something to keep Mom and Dad from fighting so much . . . If only I'd kept my room clean . . . If only . . . If only . . . If only I'd done something differently, Mom and Dad would still be together!*

Noted Christian counselor H. Norman Wright explains more about why a child of divorce (in this case, a daughter) needs to address this issue of self-forgiveness. He says:

Why forgive yourself? There are numerous reasons. You may be blaming yourself and feeling guilty for:

- not being able to change—or cure—your father;
- not living up to his spoken expectations for you;
- not being loved and accepted by him, which you attributed to a defect in your appearance or personality;
- not being perfect in some way or every way;
- treating yourself the way your father treated you;
- mistreating yourself when you have difficult times;
- choosing men like your father in hopes that you can reform them;
- developing some of the same tendencies or problems you despise in your father.

We often take out our frustrations, not on the person who hurt us, but on ourselves. We do this because we subconsciously consider ourselves a safer target. . . . After all, your father has hurt you in the past. . . . So you take the path of least resistance by shouldering the blame.[6]

Sadly, what often happens to people like you and me is that, in the end, we simply feel like we don't *deserve* God's overpowering forgiveness. Friend, I've got news for you . . . we don't! There is absolutely nothing we could ever do to deserve the amazing grace that God has chosen to heap on us! You can't earn it and you can't take out a payment plan ("Lord, if you forgive me, I'll spend the rest of my life feeding the poor in Zimbabwe").

Let's face it. We are sinners. Our parents' divorce didn't make us that, but it does magnify our sin in some ways. In spite of that, God has chosen to flood our lives with the restoring power of his forgiveness. The only thing that keeps you and me from experiencing that power is you and me ourselves.

One of my favorite one-act plays is a story written by Paul Lessard called *Debtors Prison*.[7] (Now, I have to warn you that if you've never seen or read this play, I'm about to ruin the ending for you.)

Debtors Prison is set in some unknown medieval location, and it follows the stories of three men, Duncan, William, and Terry. For one reason or another, these peasants have been locked away in jail until they can repay large, outstanding debts they incurred earlier in life.

Duncan and William are veterans of this system—they've been here for years! Used to the bleakness of their condition, they while away the days playing game after game of checkers. (With 2,346 wins, William leads the competition over Duncan's 1,998 victories.)

Terry is the newcomer. Crop failure two years in a row devastated his family's financial abilities and landed him in the Dunsmire Debtors Prison. At first, Terry is motivated by the guard's suggestion that he can work off his debt there in the prison. After all, he's got a wife and kids to support, so he needs to get out as quickly as possible.

One year later—after working fifteen-hour days nearly seven days a week—Terry asks the jailer how far along he's come in paying off his debts. The answer is not what he expected to hear. Returning sorrowfully to the cell that he shares with Duncan and William, he finally sees the hopelessness of his situation.

"Well?" says William when he sees Terry walk in.

"Rags, it's all just rags," mourns Terry. "He said all I've done is like filthy rags. My work amounts to nothing. I'll be here until I die! I owe more than when I came."

Duncan merely shrugs. "We told you not to expect so much. In debtors prison you can't pay for your own debts."

So the three resign themselves to a lifetime of imprisonment, but Terry still holds out a flicker of hope that someone, somewhere will come to redeem him. Enlisting William's aid, he writes a letter to a man known for his generosity, the Duke of Northumberland. They describe their plight and beg the duke's mercy.

Months later a letter arrives from the duke's estate. It seems he has recently passed away, and in his will he left instructions for his fortune to be used to pay off the debts of all in Dunsmire Debtors Prison!

The prisoners are beside themselves with joy. "My friends, we'll be free; we *are* free! Our debt is paid!" says William. "The door is open. Prisoners are running all over out there. Duncan, Terry, let us gather our possessions and go home!"

Laughing with joy, William and Terry make their way to the door, then notice Duncan has not joined them. In fact he hasn't moved from the table where he is plotting strategy for yet another checkers game.

William turns back and calls gently, "Duncan?" No response.

Terry adds, "The door is open; we're free to go."

Still Duncan remains unmoved. Firmly but not harshly, he speaks. "No one is interested in paying my debt. It's my concern. No one cares."

"Ah, but that's no longer true, my friend. The death of one man has brought freedom for us all," William says to his friend. "Duncan, please come."

Refusing to look at the open door before him, Duncan simply replies, "I think not. You go."

And so Terry and William march out to freedom, while Duncan remains a prisoner in a jail cell with open doors.

How often are we like that with our heavenly Father? Our God has forgiven us completely the debt of our wrongdoings; he has flung open wide the gates of sin that held us captive for so long. We've seen with our own eyes the freedom that gives to others. Yet we, like Duncan, convince ourselves that we are undeserving of that kind of mercy. So we rot in the prison of unforgiveness, refusing to allow God's great grace to penetrate our hearts so that we can actually forgive ourselves as well.

Neil Anderson says:

> The point is, Jesus saved us by bearing our sins upon Himself, therefore there is no condemnation, because we are forgiven.
>
> It has been said that 75 percent of all mentally disturbed people would be pronounced well if they could only be convinced that they are forgiven. Many seemingly healthy Christians find it difficult to believe that they are really free from condemnation. . . . There is no condemnation for the sins of the past or for the sins of the future because we are *in Christ.* . . . Does this mean we never sin? Of course not, but we don't *have* to sin, and when we do, we are not condemned.[8]

Yes, you've fallen short. Yes, you do not deserve God's liberating forgiveness in your life. Take it anyway. That, my friend, is your Father's desire for you. Why put it off? Accept and experience his grace today and every day between now and eternity!

Your Father's Forgiveness Empowers You to Forgive Your Parents

A few years ago I was fortunate enough to interview pastor and author Max Lucado for an article I was writing. As we spoke, he said something in passing that has stayed with me for years: "Never underestimate the power of God's forgiveness."[9]

I'm just now learning that what Max shared means more than the awesome potential of forgiveness *within* my life; it also encompasses the life-altering force of forgiveness *extending from* my life.

You see, there is a side benefit to succumbing fully to God's redeeming grace for you. Doing so enables you to extend grace to others who have hurt you—namely, your own parents who let their divorce inscribe lasting scars on your life.

It is easy to look back and condemn our parents for their failures in marriage and to judge how their actions have brought unwanted results over the years. It is much harder—but also much more rewarding—to look back and forgive them.

I think Oscar Wilde hit the nail on the head when he said, "Children begin by loving their parents; as they grow older they judge them; sometimes they forgive them."[10]

I think we are tempted at times to take some kind of "revenge" on our parents for the hardships we endured. Perhaps we return the distant father's favor and, when we are grown, cut ourselves off completely from him. Maybe we hold back our own children from their grandparents, justifying our actions by thinking to ourselves, *Well, they don't deserve access to my kids.* Perhaps we hold them in open contempt or look for ways to spend their money as "pay-back" for what we missed out on as kids. But when we give in to that kind of temptation, we do not honor our heavenly Father or ourselves. We simply inflict harm for harm.

As Francis Bacon reminds us, "In taking revenge a man is but even with his enemy. But in passing it over he is superior, for it is a prince's part to pardon."[11]

Let me make one thing clear here and now, though. Forgiving your parents is certainly no easy task. In fact this kind of forgiveness must often be more than a one time event; it is typically a lifetime process. We begin with the past, releasing the right to hurt back for hurt they caused us before, during, and after their divorce. Then we must continually reaffirm our forgiveness of them as their actions today may again touch a raw nerve or strike a sore emotional spot.

Does that mean we should simply allow an unkind or mean-spirited or even abusive parent to freely cause us harm? Of course not. But it does mean we make a deliberate choice not to seek ways to strike back or gain some measure of revenge for the hurt.

No, this isn't easy. But by the power of God's grace, it is more than doable—and the doing of it actually draws us closer to our heavenly Father. Why? Because it requires God's strength to forgive the one who has hurt us.

Now, there's another reason why it's wise to forgive your parents, to allow God's powerful grace to flow into, and then out of, you. It's a selfish reason, really. Author and actress Nancy Stafford explains it this way:

> No matter what people do to us, we are responsible to forgive them from our hearts, as God has forgiven us, and to repent of any of our own sinful reactions to whatever was done to us. We will never heal and really become whole until we stop blaming others or our circumstances for our pain.
>
> The hurt I feel may still be present, but as I forgive, I begin to view the incident from God's perspective, and a unique

thing takes place: I gain insight into it. It's no longer just about me; I begin to see the pain and brokenness in the lives of those who have wounded me. And I find that the more I see the things that I do and recognize my own sin and weakness, the more I begin to understand why others act the way they do.[12]

You see, when we learn to extend this forgiveness of God to our parents, it does more than just improve their lives. It improves our own lives as well. It fosters healing within, burning away the burrs of bitterness and resentment that plant themselves in our hearts. It lightens the load we must carry, lessening the pain and promoting health and well-being.

In other words, a steady regimen of forgiveness (prescribed by Dr. God) is like wellness treatments that make you a stronger, healthier, and happier person. As Samuel Johnson put it, "A wise man will make haste to forgive, because he knows the true value of time, and will not suffer it to pass away in unnecessary pain."[13]

Stanford University psychologist Carl Thoresen conducted a study to see if sentiments like Samuel Johnson's were scientifically verifiable.[14] He devised a six-session group therapy series designed to help people enact forgiveness in their lives, and enlisted 259 adults to serve as subjects for his experiment. Afterward, he discovered that people who are able to forgive are much less likely to suffer physical symptoms associated with stress and anger, such as headaches and nausea.

Thoresen checked back with his subjects six months later and found that the "positive effects" first identified when they forgave others were still present in the forgiving people's lives. Says Thoresen, "Forgiveness doesn't mean forgetting or condoning offenses, or even reconciling with the offender. It means giving up the right to be angry." The refusal to do that can haunt you, both physically and emotionally, for decades, for a lifetime.

Are you familiar with the remarkable story of Morrie Schwartz? This college professor suffered from the debilitating disease amyotrophic lateral sclerosis (ALS), commonly known as Lou Gehrig's disease. ALS eventually killed Morrie but not before he was able to spend many days with one of his old students, Mitch Albom.

One such day, as Mitch was massaging his professor's paralyzed legs and feet, Morrie revealed one major regret of his otherwise fulfilling life. Many years before, he had refused to forgive a friend for a wrong.

Morrie's friend Norman was an artist. Thirty years prior, the friend had sculpted a bust of Morrie—a sculpture that still held a place of prominence in the Schwartz home. But soon after, Norman and his wife moved away to another city. Several months later Morrie's wife underwent a serious surgery. Although Norman and his family knew about it, they neglected to contact the Schwartzes to offer condolence and support. And Morrie never forgave his friend for that slight.

Decades later, as his own death from ALS drew near, Morrie's thoughts returned to that unforgiveness. "Over the years, I met Norman a few times and he always tried to reconcile, but I didn't accept it," Morrie said. "A few years ago . . . he died of cancer. I feel so sad. I never got to see him. I never got to forgive. It pains me now so much."

With tears in his eyes, Morrie gave his student one last lesson. "Forgive yourself," he said. "Forgive others. Don't wait, Mitch. Not everyone gets the time I'm getting. Not everyone is as lucky."[15]

Friend, don't wait until you too are near death to realize that regret comes with unforgiveness. Learn the lesson that Morrie Schwartz taught to Mitch Albom, and apply it to your relationship with your parents. Determine now to take the forgiveness that God spills in abundance on you and splash some of it toward Mom and Dad.

Believe me when I say this: You need to give grace to your parents as much—maybe more—than they need to receive it. Author James Emery White wisely said:

> Failing to forgive not only saddles you with a heavy burden, it also brings bondage. It holds you captive by poisoning your emotions and then giving those damaged emotions control of your life. The wrong you suffered prevents you from moving forward with your life. It consumes you, and only forgiveness can break the cycle.[16]

Do yourself a favor. Break the cycle and start the process of forgiveness today.

Your Father's Forgiveness Never Runs Out

I want you to understand one last thing about your Father's forgiveness before we end this chapter. It is this: God's grace toward you never runs out. There is no expiration date on his forgiveness, no emptying of the bottle that washes away your sins and empowers you to forgive others.

There is a story about a poor country doctor who was known both for his skill in medicine and for his Christlike character.[17] On the good doctor's death, his wife opened the accounting books from his practice and was surprised to see several entries crossed out in red ink. Next to each billing amount, the doctor's red pen had written, "Forgiven—too poor to pay."

The man's wife was furious. Her husband had earned that money legitimately, and she was determined that those debts be paid. She immediately filed a lawsuit in court, demanding payment from the forgiven debtors. She asked the judge to reinstate the debts that the old doctor had kindly erased.

During the court proceedings, the judge asked to look at the accounting books. Gazing through the pages, he asked, "Is this your husband's handwriting in red?"

"Yes," the woman replied.

"Then," the judge ruled, "not a court in the land can obtain the money from those whom he has forgiven." With that, he dismissed the lawsuit.

There are times in this life when our enemy, the devil, sneaks up close and begins to whisper lies in our ears. "Remember that sin you committed last week? Well, you committed it again today—twice! God forgave you once, sure. Maybe even twice. But that third time was one too many. How could he forgive you now? Surely he is sick of forgiving you for that same sin over and over! Yes, perhaps now his grace has finally run out . . ."

Don't allow yourself to be fooled by lies like this! You must understand, God's grace never grows weak, never gets watered down, never runs out. That runs counter to our own natural instincts, doesn't it? Yet that's why it's a good thing that he is God and we are not!

Listen, friend, if there were only one truth you could take to heart from this chapter, this is what I would wish it to be. Our natural tendency is to rush to judgment; God's natural tendency is to forgive. That's his character, his personality. Your Father is not who he is because he forgives; he forgives every wrong that you have done or will do—past, present, and future—because of who he is.

There is a corollary to this truth of God's never-ending grace for you. Not only does your Father always forgive, he also promises to forget. What an amazing ability this is! God, in his infinite power, can voluntarily limit his own omniscience on your behalf. He can do what you cannot—forgive your sin and then forget about it.

I love the way Pastor Max Lucado brings this concept home, so much so that I'm going to let his eloquent words close out this chapter.

I was thanking the Father today for His mercy. I began listing the sins He'd forgiven. One by one I thanked God for forgiving my stumbles and tumbles. My motives were pure and my heart was thankful. But my understanding of God was wrong. It was when I used the word remember that it hit me.

"Remember the time I . . ." I was about to thank God for another act of mercy. But I stopped. Something was wrong. The word remember seemed displaced. It was an off-key note in a sonata, a misspelled word in a poem. It was a baseball game in December. It didn't fit. . . .

Then I remembered. I remembered His words, "And I will remember their sins no more" (Hebrews 8:12). . . . God doesn't just forgive, He forgets. He erases the board. He destroys the evidence. He burns the microfilm. He clears the computer.

He doesn't remember my mistakes. For all the things He does do, this is one thing He refuses to do. He refuses to keep a list of my wrongs. . . .

Do yourself a favor. Purge your cellar. Exorcise your basement. Take the Roman nails of Calvary and board up the door.

And remember . . . He forgot.[18]

Something to Think About . . .

Use the following questions either by yourself or with a group to process what you've learned in this chapter.

- When have you felt, without a doubt, the forgiveness of God working in your life?
- Why do you suppose it's sometimes hard to forgive ourselves for our failures?
- What are the top three things for which your parents most need your forgiveness? How can you begin the forgiveness process for those things today?
- When do you feel like God's grace has "run out" in your life? What can you do to realign your feelings with the truth?

Something to Do

Open your Bible and spend a half hour or so reading the following Scripture verses. Pause after each passage and whisper to yourself the words, "This promise is for *me.*" Keep reading and whispering until it finally sinks in that you—yes, *you!*—have a heavenly Father who is always ready, able, and willing to forgive you and restore you to a fulfilling relationship with him and the other children in his family.

- 1 John 1:9
- Hebrews 8:12
- Ephesians 1:7–8
- Psalm 103:12
- Isaiah 1:19

Hungry for more? Then check out these additional Bible passages.

- Luke 15:11–32
- Ephesians 4:32
- Luke 17:3–4
- Matthew 18:23–35
- Luke 7:36–50
- Psalm 86:5
- Colossians 1:12–14

7

A Father Who Comforts You

Earlier this month the leaders at my church decided it was time for a "change-up" of sorts, time to do something a little different during the Sunday morning meeting. So, instead of the typical format, we held a "celebration service."

The purpose of this celebration was simply to take some time to reflect on the goodness of God in our lives, to "breathe" for a bit, and let our eyes and hearts focus on our Father's care for us. As a deliberate part of that morning, there wasn't much of a sermon. Instead, my pastor, Kent Hummel, delivered a few words of wisdom, then turned the microphone over to others for a time of testimony.

I have to tell you, it was one of the most refreshing church services I've attended in some time. I enjoyed it so much, in fact, that as we enter this chapter and begin our discussion of the comforting goodness of our Father in our lives, I've decided to share that experience (in my own small way) with you here.

Friend, there's much to say about God's compassionate presence in the lives of people like you and me, people who've felt the loss of a parent and the hardships that follow. But instead of "preaching a sermon" to you right now, I think what we both need is a celebration time, a period of testimonies and reflection that allows us to see—not just hear about—God's gentle hand at work in the lives of people.

I think, then, this will be a chapter of stories—of testimonies regarding God's comfort—with a few words of wisdom sprinkled in here and there.

And so I urge you now to sit back, relax, and allow these stories to enable you to drink in the goodness of your Father. And may we all take comfort in the warmth of his gentle goodness toward you and me.

A baby was crying somewhere. No, not just crying, this child had filled its lungs with fistfuls of oxygen and now expelled that air with a raging wail that spoke what words could not—fear, cold, confusion, pain. The baby was crying all right. And it took more than a moment for it to sink in that he was doing it in my arms.

He had traveled some distance in a short time. Only hours ago, he had lain in peaceful darkness, sheltered from harm within the nurturing home of his mother's womb. Then came the changes as his little home began to move him toward the exit. Somewhere along the way, his supply of life-giving oxygen was restricted and his little heartbeat plummeted, sending panicked doctors and nurses flying around a hospital—and his parents into prayer.

Within twenty minutes, he had been forcibly removed from his comfortable home, delivered into the world via caesarean section surgery. Here he found plenty of oxygen—and nothing familiar, nothing that he liked!

Now his mother was recovering from surgery and the nurses, unable to comfort him, had placed the newborn boy—my son—in my arms. And he cried.

I stared at his perfect little form, at a complete loss as to what to do. After all, how does a man who never had a father know what a father is supposed to do with a screaming infant? I looked for help toward the nurse, but she had already turned away. I tried rocking his tiny body, but still he wailed.

Finally I spoke, "It's okay, Tony," I said quietly. "You're okay . . ."

And a miracle happened. At the first rumblings of sound from my throat, my boy choked back a sob. The longer I spoke, the more he seemed to listen. In seconds his breathing shallowed and evened out, his tiny chest heaved less and less. In a minute he was calm, nearly silent, focusing all his senses on the sound of my voice.

All too soon, the moment passed and another nurse returned to take the child away for tests and footprints and who knows what else. But for a brief instant, all it took to comfort my child was the sound of his father's voice.

I understood later that all the while Tony was in his mother's womb, he could hear what was going on outside. Over the months leading to his birth, he had grown accustomed to my voice—heard me singing on the couch next to his mother while I tried to teach myself guitar, heard me laughing, whispering sweet nothings, and who knows what else. When he was abruptly delivered into the world of people, the shock was overwhelming. But when I began to speak comfort to him, even though he didn't understand a word I said, the voice he heard was one he knew. It carried the reassurance of home, the security of a father.

Sometimes, I must admit, I feel much like that newborn child I once held. My world has changed without notice, casting me into a scary, noisy, cold, unknown place. As a younger man, my soul used to flail and scream just like a child, and to be honest, it still does from time to time.

But now I'm learning something else. If I will pause, catch my breath, strain my ears, I can hear his voice. You know whose—my heavenly Father's voice, whispering, cajoling, reminding me, "It's okay. You're okay. I'm right here with you like I always have been. It's all going to be okay . . ."

Oh, that I could learn to listen more! For there is always comfort in the sound of my Father's voice.

[Jesus said,] "I will pray the Father, and He will give you another Helper, that He may abide with you forever, even the Spirit of truth, whom the world cannot receive, because it neither sees Him nor knows Him; but you know Him, for He dwells with you and will be in you. I will not leave you orphans; I will come to you."

John 14:16–18 NKJV

The Greek word which is translated comforter [or "helper" in John 14] is *parakletos.* It is seen in our English word, "paraclete," which literally means "one who is called alongside."

In secular Greek the term "paraclete" has several interesting uses. Most basically, it meant one who is called to someone's aid. . . . This gave way to a more specific meaning, one who appears on behalf of another person, as a lawyer in a court case. Finally, the word came to mean an intercessor, mediator, or helper. . . . In Christian use the word means one who encourages, exhorts, appeals, or gives comfort or consolation.

Wayne A. Detzler[1]

107

To be honest, Joyce Martin McCollough was ready to leave. Members of the award-winning southern gospel trio The Martins, Joyce and her two siblings had gathered at their record company's office building to preview new songs in the hope of finding a few to go on their new album.[2]

Looking back on that day of listening to songs in Phil Johnson's office, big sister Joyce admits, "We were not really in the best of moods. And we were not really agreeing about song selection and all that."

Finally, Phil said, "I have one more song to play you." Then he cued up a song written by Scott Krippayne and Steve Siler called, "More Like a Whisper."

To be honest, little sis Judy Martin Hess wasn't listening all that closely. She and Joyce almost let this song pass by. Then she noticed Jonathan, the brother in the middle of the two girls, weeping quietly as he listened. Immediately Judy and Joyce tuned in to the song as well.

The lyrics of the chorus rang out, "When questions rain down like thunder/Sometimes the answer is more like a whisper . . ."

With tears rolling down his face as the song ended, Jonathan said, "That makes me think about Taylor."

Taylor Martin, Jonathan's son, is one-half of a twin package that arrived in the lives of Jonathan and his wife, Melinda, on New Year's Eve 1995. The proud mom and dad were thrilled to welcome Taylor and his brother Michael into the world—but were worried as well. You see, the twins weren't expected to be born until March of 1996. As you know, any child born two-and-a-half months premature can suffer complications.

Both babies struggled at birth, and doctors weren't sure either would survive. Family and friends prayed, and somehow the boys gained strength and were eventually allowed to go home with a clean bill of health. No one knew anything was still wrong with Taylor until just over a year later, February of 1997.

Michael had begun sitting up and crawling and doing all the things babies do, but Taylor still was not progressing in his development. Tests revealed that Taylor had brain damage—the crippling disease cerebral palsy.

Jonathan and Melinda, along with their extended families and scores of fans, immediately began praying for healing, asking God to restore health to this child. In concert after concert across the country, Jonathan shared about his sons and requested prayer for Taylor. Deep inside, Jonathan hoped for a miracle of the mountain-moving kind, something grand and complete, his child transformed by the healing power of God.

But sometimes miracles don't come in that shape and size. Sometimes they're more like a whisper.

When Taylor was around eighteen months old, he did something doctors weren't sure he'd ever do. He began to speak.

Yes, he still had cerebral palsy. Yes, he was still unable to walk. Yes, he still had difficulty moving his lower body and his arms. But he did begin to speak.

Jonathan reports, "He says, 'Dada' and 'Mama' and 'Papa.' But he also says the name of Jesus, which is for us a very, very special thing."

If Taylor is able to speak, then it's possible he will walk and grow and eventually be able to live a generally normal life, despite his disability. Taylor's voice became a whispered answer to Jonathan's prayer, a whispered breath of hope.

Jonathan explains, "God didn't just heal Taylor, but through Taylor's improving and starting to speak, that little one-and-a-half-year-old voice speaking 'Daddy' and saying 'Jesus' and saying 'I love you' confirmed in my heart that 'Hey! This is your answer. This is God saying everything's going to be all right.'"

Back in the record company's office, Judy said to Phil Johnson, "We've got to listen to that one again." Dutifully, Phil cued up the tape of "More Like a Whisper" once more. When the song ended this time, there wasn't a dry eye in the room.

As you can guess, "More Like a Whisper" made the album. You can hear it for yourself on The Martins' CD, *Dream Big.* If you're a fan of The Martins, you'll notice something special about this song. The trio opted not to sing it in their trademark three-part harmony style. Instead, Jonathan sings it solo, telling the world that sometimes God's comfort is more like a whisper, a whisper he's heard for himself.

In the weeks that followed the 9/11 terrorist attacks, several Christian publications contacted me for comments because they knew I was both an Arab-American and a Christian. As I searched for wisdom to comfort both my readers and myself in the wake of this national tragedy, this story was born. It is a story about a man who lost something or someone very dear—no one knows for sure just what. And in the losing of that someone or something, he also lost hope.

The man left his home and traveled far and wide in search of his missing hope. He visited the hallowed halls of government, observing the political giants and brilliant statesmen of his time. He was buoyed for a bit then. But all too soon he noticed these great leaders were also mere humans, people subject to failings just like he was. There was no real comfort to be found here.

Next he sought out the military stations of his great nation. He took pride in the swollen ranks of men and women willing to die for his country. He counted the missiles and admired the strategic, brute strength of weapons and armies. But somewhere in the sea of soldiers and guns, he realized this hope too could only be temporary, carried in the hands of imperfect humans like him. That thought left him cold and comfortless as well.

So the man went to the banking institutions, standing in awe of their time-tested financial power and admiring the majesty of their gold-plated buildings and lead-lined vaults. He marveled at the monetary transactions that laid foundations for businesses and homes, wars and fortunes, and more. Yet, after a while, he blinked and then all he saw was paper changing hands. This too was only a short-lived comfort, a temporary hope.

Sadly, the man returned home, empty-handed and empty-hearted. There he found a surprise. The Son of God himself sat in his living room. "I wondered when you'd get here," he said.

"Who are you?" the man asked.

"I am your Hope, your Comfort, your Future."

The Son opened nail-scarred palms to the man, and within them he found what he'd always needed—hope that rests not in the twisted, deformed ways of humanity but in the unwavering, everlasting grip of Jesus Christ.

So, then, how can we as believers gain comfort in this war-weary world of misguided hopes? The answer is easy but it's impossible for us sin-soaked humans to do, without help from God's empowering Holy Spirit. We must throw ourselves recklessly into the comforting strength of the nail-scarred hands that hold our only true, eternal hope. Only there can we find that which we have lost; only there can we reclaim the security and comfort that is so easily taken by the unholy circumstances of yesterday, of today, and tomorrow.

The Lord has come to wipe away our tears. He is doing it; He will have it done as soon as He can; and until He can, He would have them flow without bitterness; to which end He tells us it is a blessed thing to mourn, because of the comfort on its way. Accept His comfort now, and so prepare for the comfort at hand. He is getting you ready for it, but you must be a fellow worker with Him. . . .

God is the God of comfort, known of man as the refuge, the life-giver, or not known at all. . . . Let us comfort ourselves in the thought of the Father and the Son. So long as there dwells harmony, so long as the Son loves the Father with all the love the Father can welcome, all is well with the little ones.

George MacDonald[3]

Then I saw a new heaven and a new earth, for the first heaven and the first earth had passed away, and the sea was no more. And I saw the holy city, new Jerusalem, coming down out of heaven from God, prepared as a bride adorned for her husband. And I heard a loud voice from the throne saying, "Behold, the dwelling place of God is with man. He will dwell with them, and they will be His people, and God Himself will be with them as their God. He will wipe away every tear from their eyes, and death shall be no more, neither shall there be mourning nor crying nor pain anymore, for the former things have passed away."

Revelation 21:1–4 ESV

In 1985 it would have been futile to say to Sue Sawyer, "You worry about life too much. It has no meaning. Relax and enjoy it."

Sue couldn't do that. She worked as a nurse in an intensive care unit at her hospital. Every day she was confronted with patients who were staring death in the face. If she wasn't thinking about it, they were.

Two individuals are etched on Sue's mind. One was an LOL. That's an acronym medical people use for endearing *little old ladies*. This LOL was in Sue's unit just a short time.

One day this LOL clicked on her call light and Sue was the only nurse available to respond. Sue said, "I went in, even though she was not my patient that day. I so clearly remember entering and asking her what she wanted. 'You're not my patient today. Do you want me to get your nurse?' I asked. I knew how much LOLs like to talk and that day I was busy."

The lady responded to Sue's inquiry, "I want to tell you something."

Sue protested, "I'm not your nurse. I'll go and get her."

But the lady was insistent. "No need for that. I just wanted to tell *you* something. Now shut the door, honey." (Sue knew that she was in for a long talk. *Arrgh,* she thought. *Oh, well. I bet the hours pass by too slowly for her. I guess I can listen for a bit. Poor thing.*)

The lady took Sue's hand and said succinctly, "I know I'm dying. I have waited my whole life to see Jesus, and now I will see him soon. I am so excited." She paused, patted my hand, and then squeezed it. "That's all I want to say, honey."

Sue muttered, "Isn't that wonderful!" and left feeling puzzled and troubled.

Later she witnessed a man's death. He was one of the World War II vets who had been a boxer in the Air Force. "I stood outside his room and watched," Sue recalled. "As his blood pressure and heart rate began to decelerate, he started wildly swinging his arms in the air. He must have thought he was losing consciousness during a boxing match. The picture spoke *so* loudly, it was *so* symbolic. I stood transfixed, watching. The man was raging against the 'dying of the light.' He was so different from the lady I had talked to the previous week."

Death came for both the LOL and the boxer. Yet, for that little lady, death didn't come alone. Alongside it was God's gentle comfort, warming her soul and preparing her for a long-awaited homecoming in heaven.

For the boxer, there was no comfort in death, no respite, no relief, only death.

Sue went home that night deeply troubled by the boxer's death. She thought, "He was so different from the little lady. I wonder which way *I* will face death—at peace, the way the little old lady did, or swinging wildly, fighting against the unknown, the way the boxer did."

The soil of Sue's heart had been well prepared by the two concurrent events. A few days later her friend Diane invited her to a spaghetti dinner. As they chatted about many things, the matter of Sue's relationship to Jesus Christ arose. Diane told her of a heavenly Father's desire for her to spend eternity with him in heaven. That night Sue received eternal life as she placed her faith in Christ's death on her behalf.

As Sue reflected on these events, she said, "What a creative God! He orchestrated my circumstances so perfectly that they collectively wooed me to him. I'm touched by the fact that he knew how to gently call me, a sinner, to come home."[4]

God is closest to those with broken hearts.

Jewish Proverb

Christian musician John Cox still doesn't know her name, but he'll always remember the young woman who interrupted his 1995 concert in Dallas. She was just another face in the crowd until she stood up and began walking toward the stage.

Up front, John was telling a story, making his way through an elaborate introduction to his next song. Suddenly the girl was in front of him, one arm outstretched in John's direction. John wasn't sure how to react at first—after all, it's not every day you find yourself face-to-face with a fan right in the middle of your big intro!

Almost as an afterthought, John noticed the girl was holding something, a napkin. And for some reason, she was trying to hand that napkin to John. Right then.

A million thoughts must have raced through John's mind. Was he sweating too much and needed to wipe off? Did he have a smudge on his chin? Was it time to stop so the audience could eat? What?

The surprised musician finally reached for the napkin. Her delivery completed, the girl wordlessly returned to her seat for the rest of the concert. Curiosity piqued, John glanced down at the paper in his hand.

"Play the song, 'Don't Look Away.'"

He looked again. Yep, it was just a song request. But wait, there was also something more.

Captured by the moment, John nearly forgot where he was and what he was doing as he was mentally transported away, into the story the girl had scribbled on the napkin.

The year was 1992. She sat, tired and spent, in the car, waiting in the parking lot. The needle tracks that dotted her arms revealed a deadly dependence, an addiction that would either kill her or leave her constantly craving more of the substance that wreaked havoc with her mind and body.

At that moment, all she wanted to do was sit and listen. The tape, a gift from a friend, was rolling in the player. On it a rough-voiced singer and his gritty guitar spoke in a way she couldn't resist.

She turned up the volume. The song was a simple tune called "Don't Look Away." The singer, a guy named John Cox, sang with a passion she could almost touch. He told her— in so many words—she needed God.

"Every time I look around," the lyrics sang, "I start to sink and I'm swallowed by the sea." She caught her breath. *That's me!* she thought, listening harder now, hanging on every word.

Then the chorus finally came around with the words "I hear Jesus say he can't hurt you now/ Don't look away, just keep your eyes on me. . . ."

There was something about that song . . . no, there was something about the Person John was singing about. Suddenly she craved that Person, craved the comfort he could bring more than any drug, more than any alcohol, more than anything. And, she could sense it, he craved her too, longed to reach out and comfort her heart and soul, like a Father longing for his daughter to come home.

Right at that moment, alone in her car, she called out to Jesus, begging him to save her. And right at that moment, joining her in that car, Jesus did. Never again would drugs control her life. She was God's daughter, and she had come home.

Three years later, she heard that John Cox was coming to town for a concert, and she knew she had to go. At the concert, she could barely control her excitement. This talented singer had such a passion for Jesus, and God had used that passion to bring her to the Lord. But John didn't even know about it. Almost without thinking, she grabbed a napkin and scribbled a story—her story—on it. She couldn't wait; she had to give it to him now.

When John finished reading the napkin, tears began to stream down his cheeks. Time finally seemed to begin ticking once more as he remembered where he was. Looking over the audience, he finally said, "There's no way I can explain this to you now, so I'm just going to go on to the next song." And he sang, "Don't Look Away."

Reflecting on that moment later, John said in awestruck tones, "That song provided a highway for her to see God directly in front of her. As a musician, that's your highest calling right there. That just totally blew me away—and it still does."

Then, with a smile, he added in closing, "I've still got the napkin."[5]

He will listen to the prayers of the destitute. He will not reject their pleas.

Psalm 102:17 NLT

A father to the fatherless, a defender of widows, is God in his holy dwelling. God sets the lonely in families.

Psalm 68:5–6

The LORD is my shepherd, I shall not be in want. He makes me lie down in green pastures, he leads me beside quiet waters, he restores my soul.

Psalm 23:1–3

Give your burdens to the LORD, and he will take care of you. He will not permit the godly to slip and fall.

Psalm 55:22 NLT

I once interviewed renowned author and thinker Philip Yancey over lunch at a restaurant in Denver. As we talked, the conversation turned toward the difficulties of life and finding God's comfort during times of sorrow.

It was then that Philip shared a few insights about the power of the Bible—the Book of Psalms, particularly—in helping us to express and work through pain. Rather than try to summarize his thoughts, I'll let him explain it in his own words:

MN (Mike Nappa): What would you say the Psalms teach us about dealing with life's difficult circumstances, about finding comfort in times of pain?

PY (Philip Yancey): The book that was, in our time, on the *New York Times* best-seller list longer than any other book is M. Scott Peck's book, *The Road Less Traveled.* And it was on the list for eight years or something like that, and I think the reason that book struck such a chord is because of the first sentence, which is, "Life is difficult." Many of the other books on that list were saying, "Here's how to solve life," "Here's how to save your marriage," "Here's how to raise your kids," "Here's how to do all these things," and people were finding out it didn't work. Life doesn't work like that. It doesn't work according to formula. And Scott Peck had the guts to say that. He started out by saying, "Life is difficult."

What I like about the Psalms is that they reflect the reality of my life, as well as the reality of the psalmist's life. And what I learned from them is that it's okay to take that disappointment, that anger, the rage even, to God and simply express it. . . . There are some times when I feel like [the beauty of] Psalm 23. I take a walk in the mountains behind my home. I look at the wildflowers, and Psalm 23 fits. But I go back and face the stuff I'd left to take that walk, and [the pain of] Psalm 22 is there. So, again, it's the very variety and diversity that I came to rely on.

MN: Now when we take those and express those emotions to God, is that what you call "spiritual reality therapy"?

PY: Yeah. You go to any counselor for marriage problems, and the first step before you can get into any kind of cure is "You've got to let out those things that have been bottled up for years." Only if you expose a wound to the air will it heal. And that's true of emotional wounds as well.

MN: Do you think sometimes we're too timid to share that with God?

PY: Well, yeah! And the churches encourage us to be, don't they? . . . But actually, we're all going through that stuff. And the Psalms simply give us permission to be open about it. . . .

The way I learned to read Psalms was by realizing what they are. They're like somebody's spiritual journal. I don't think most of the psalm writers thought, "Oh, I think that I will record my thoughts for posterity so that three thousand years from now, Philip and Mike can take these and grow." They weren't thinking that at all. Just like you keep a spiritual journal—just like I should keep a spiritual journal—that's what these psalmists were doing. And because they were so good, the community of faith back then, the Israelites, recognized that these are sacred; these are revelation.

This is part of what God wants us to know about how to relate to him. . . . The surprise to me, as I got to know the Psalms, is that about one-half of them are what I call "wintry psalms." (I borrow that phrase from Martin Marty.) Only half of them are "summery"—bright and cheerful, sunny. Half of them are very morose. They're negative. They're melancholy. And I'm kind of that way a lot so I identify with that half. . . .

[We need to realize that] not all psalms are written for each one of us every day. They reflect the up-and-downness, the moods of life. The nice thing is they're all there and they cover all those moods, no matter what you're feeling. You can probably find a psalm that expresses that better than you could.

MN: So basically, we're a multidimensional people and through the Psalms, we discover how God can meet us in every dimension?

PY: Yeah, great way of expressing it. [Leaning toward microphone and laughing] I said that, not Mike![6]

* * *

Matt, Charlie, Steve, and Dan couldn't help but utter silent prayers for reassurance and comfort as they approached the door of the San Francisco nightclub. They were scheduled to perform there that night but quickly had second thoughts when they saw the bouncer standing at the door wearing a T-shirt that proclaimed, "666 is my favorite number."

Still, the four guys in Jars of Clay (Dan Haseltine, Steve Mason, Charlie Lowell, and Matt Odmark) had been praying for an opportunity to use their music to reach out to non-Christians. Time and again they had pleaded with God—both individually and collectively—to let them be "bridge builders," and "ground softeners" who prepare the way for Christ to come into people's lives. So, when the invitation came to play at this party spot in the city by the bay, they accepted. Despite their reservations, they determined to go through with their performance of Jesus-focused songs in this San Francisco hangout.

It was about an hour before midnight when they walked inside and saw a big goat's head—a symbol of Satan worship—prominently displayed right above the stage.

They laugh about it now, but at the time they weren't sure how to react. Dan says, "We were all pretty naive to the club scene. We didn't know *what* to expect. . . . [The goat's head] showed us that this is *not* a place where Christians frequent! I think we were all really scared about how people were going to react to what we were doing and things we were singing."

Nervously at first, the guys began their set. They all wanted nothing more than just to pack up and leave! As if on cue, barely into the first song, a fight broke out in the back of the bar. Trying to calm their shaking nerves, the four young men continued singing, praying for God's Spirit to take over and bring peace to the room.

They sang, and stone-faced drinkers stared back up at them—or simply ignored them altogether. Still they sang, performing hit tunes like "Love Song for a Savior" and "Flood."

Slowly, almost imperceptibly at first, the hush began to fall over the nightclub. Trickling bit by bit through the strings, keyboards, and lyrics, the message of the music started penetrating the hearts of those who previously ignored it. God was present, moving quietly in the club, calming and comforting the nervous players, answering the silent prayers of the band members who had asked to be vehicles of his love to a lost and dying world.

"By the end of the set," Dan says, "the transformation that took place from the beginning of the show to the end of the show was so obvious. It was amazing just to watch the faces turn from very stone-cold to transparent. It was intense that night."

Steve adds, "We were so afraid and there were so many variables involved. It was obvious this was one of those places where God wanted us to trust him. . . . We were kind of ill at ease because we knew we were right there where the Word and the world were colliding and we were watching it happen."

From that point on, the band reports, the comfort of knowing they were fulfilling God's purpose in their lives brought a new prayer to their lips—a prayer of praise and deeper commitment. "Okay, God," Steve remembers praying, "we know this is what you want us to do. You've worked here and shown us that if we're obedient to this calling, then you have work to do in these people's lives."[7]

And God continues to do that work today through a musical treasure found in Jars of Clay.

> For whatever things were written before were written for our learning, that we through the patience and comfort of the Scriptures might have hope.
>
> Romans 15:4 NKJV

> Blessed be the God and Father of our Lord Jesus Christ, the Father of mercies and God of all comfort, who comforts us in all our affliction, so that we will be able to comfort those who are in any affliction with the comfort with which we ourselves are comforted by God.
>
> 2 Corinthians 1:3–4 NASB

> For the Lord Himself will descend from heaven with a shout, with the voice of the archangel and with the trumpet of God, and the dead in Christ will rise first. Then we who are alive and remain will be caught up together with them in the clouds to meet the Lord in the air, and so we shall always be with the Lord. Therefore comfort one another with these words.
>
> 1 Thessalonians 4:16–18 NASB

> For when we came into Macedonia, this body of ours had no rest, but we were harassed at every turn—conflicts on the outside, fears within. But God, who comforts the downcast, comforted us.
>
> 2 Corinthians 7:5–6

Deep down, in my heart of hearts, I know this: Even if there are no Under Construction signs, no tracks from heavy machinery, no sounds of heavenly jackhammers in the background, the Master Architect and Builder is always hard at work in the lives of his children.

God is aware of your circumstances and moves among them. God is aware of your pain and monitors every second of it.

God is aware of your emptiness and seeks to fill it in a manner beyond your dreams.

God is aware of your wounds and scars and knows how to draw forth a healing deeper than you can imagine.

Even when your situation seems out of control.

Even when you feel alone and afraid.

God works the night shift.

Ron Mehl[8]

Recently I worked on a humorous video short called "Praying Lucy." Chances are good you'll never see this one, so I'm going to tell you about it here.

The film starts with a soccer tryout. A teenage girl, Lucy, is giving it her best, but her best still falls woefully short. She's humiliated out there and, as one would expect, doesn't make the team. Afterward, she forlornly packs up her gear and prays to God for a little comfort and consolation.

"You know, God," she says, "I'm really pretty discouraged about this whole situation . . . God, if you really love me, just give me a sign. Some kind of encouragement to help me feel better and know you care, okay?"

And so she trudges on through the rest of her day. At home later, the phone rings, and sad little Lucy picks it up. It's her mother, calling to check on the tryout. Mom reminds Lucy that she's good at other things besides soccer and tries cheering her with the news that Lucy is her favorite daughter in the whole world.

Lucy just rolls her eyes and says, "You have to say stuff like that. You're my mom."

The conversation ends and Lucy continues her prayer. "Anyway, God, I could sure use that encouragement, you know? So anytime you want to . . ."

Dingdong! Lucy's prayer is interrupted by a mail delivery at the front door. It's a card, just for her, sent by her best friend. She reads, "Dear Lucy, I was just thinking about you and decided to write you a note to tell you how special you are to me . . . Blah blah blah . . ."

Without thinking, the poor girl dumps the letter in the wastebasket and resumes her prayer. "Anyway, God . . . I could sure use an encouraging word or two, you know? Something to remind me that you love me and all . . ."

Unexpectedly, a Bible falls off the shelf overhead, conks Lucy on the noggin, and then falls open in front of her on a desk. You guessed it, the book lands open to reveal an encouraging word from Scripture. Lucy reads it, shrugs it off, and continues her prayer for God to somehow, some way, send her a little comfort to help her feel better!

The doorbell rings again, and it's Barney, the mail carrier, returned. He noticed Lucy's soccer uniform and came back to let her know that his daughter is coaching a new soccer team and needs players. Lucy, however, is caught up in her own sorrows.

"What? Oh, sorry, Barney," she says. "I wasn't paying attention." She takes all her soccer equipment and throws it in the garbage outside. Finally she turns to Barney and says, "What a rotten day! I guess God doesn't love me after all."

And before Barney can say another word, she leaves him at the curb and walks unhappily back inside.

Poor Lucy. God, in his goodness, had sent his comforting presence to her through her family, friends, the Bible, and even the mail carrier! But Lucy is so wrapped up in feeling miserable, she doesn't even notice and then mistakenly assumes God doesn't really care after all![9]

You know why I'm telling you this story, don't you? I can see the glint of understanding in your eyes.

Yes, we too are often like Lucy. Caught up in the daily grind of disappointing circumstances, we call out to God for help and comfort, then don't bother to notice when he hand delivers it to our hearts!

Friend, after experiencing life without one, you now have at your disposal a Father who can *and will* bring comfort to your soul. When he comes with comfort today, promise yourself that you won't miss it.

Something to Think About . . .

Use the following questions either by yourself or with a group to process what you've learned in this chapter.

- How did it make you feel to read about others who have experienced God's comforting presence in their lives? Explain.
- In what ways does God reach out to comfort his children today? When have you experienced comfort in one or more of those ways?
- What keeps you from finding regular comfort in the Scriptures? What can you do about that?
- This week, how can you get better at recognizing God's comforting hand at work in your daily circumstances?

Something to Do

Write the following Scripture passage on a 3x5 card:

Blessed be the God and Father of our Lord Jesus Christ, the Father of mercies and God of all comfort, who comforts us in all our affliction.

2 Corinthians 1:3–4 NASB

Put the card in your purse, wallet, or pocket. At least five times today, take the card out and whisper the words to yourself until you believe them!

8

A Father Who
Challenges You

"You give them something to eat."

The challenge must have made Andrew, Peter, and the other apostles gulp involuntarily. Yet the words hung in the air, the matter-of-fact command delivered without remorse or even an acknowledgment that what Jesus had just asked of his disciples was actually impossible.[1]

You give them something to eat.

I imagine that Andrew started doing the math first, adding up the number of people in this group over here and that group over there and multiplying to find an estimated crowd count.

Fifty . . . one hundred . . . one thousand . . . five thousand! And that's only the men. I'm afraid to even count up all the women and children!

One day's wage could buy enough bread to feed around twenty-five men. That meant to even begin to feed this crowd just once would take nearly a year's wages! Yet here was Jesus calmly telling his followers to start the food flowing. Couldn't he add? Did he have a secret stash of slush money they didn't know about? Or was he trying to give them all migraine headaches just for fun?

It had all started earlier in the day. Ready for a little solitude, Jesus had led his followers out to what the Bible describes as "a desolate place." The only trouble was that townspeople had seen Jesus leave and they raced ahead of him to this desolate place. By the time Jesus and his disciples arrived, the place was packed with people, all wanting to hear more from the Christ. So Jesus did what he always does; he made time for them. He sat among them and taught them many things about the Father.

Finally, the hour became late, and the disciples were ready to go, probably hungry themselves. Checking the time, they inched up to Jesus and suggested he wrap things up. "Send them away," they said, motioning to the thousands who made up Jesus' audience, "to go into the surrounding countryside and villages and buy themselves something to eat."

I picture Jesus pausing to look over the crowd, then with the hint of a smile on his face, issuing the challenge that came next. "You give them something to eat."

I wonder if Thomas's heart skipped a beat just then. Or if Peter might have uttered an exclamation under his breath. Or if they all just got that deer-in-the-headlights, panicked look that so often accompanies an overwhelming task.

The Bible records that the disciples responded with shock. "Shall we go and buy two hundred denarii worth of bread and give it to them to eat?" (A denarius was a day's wage for a laborer.)

Of course, I like the MNU (Mike Nappa Unabridged) translation of this passage better: "Are you CRAZY, Jesus? Can't you see there are THOUSANDS AND THOUSANDS of people here? Even if we HAD money, it would take two hundred days' worth of wages to buy enough bread to feed this mob. Surely you don't mean what you just said . . . Do you?"

Well, at least that's what I would've said. But Jesus is unconcerned. He, it seems, knows something the rest of us don't—and he's about to prove it. "How many loaves do you have?" he cajoles. "Go and see."

The report comes back that their little company has a grand total of five loaves of bread and two small fish.

Now, it's obvious. What Jesus has asked for is not just impractical, it is impossible. With men, that is.

The challenge is nothing for God. With what must have been a "no biggie" shrug of his shoulders, Jesus commanded the meal to begin. He instructed the people in the crowd to sit down in groups of fifty and one hundred. Then he said a blessing and divided the bread and fish among his disciples. Each one took his pitiful share and began serving the groups seated in the countryside . . . and kept serving . . . and kept handing out more food and more food. A miracle had happened! The food never ran out! In fact there was enough for everyone in the crowd to eat his or her fill. And, as if for good measure, Jesus finished the meal by commanding Andrew and Peter and the rest to go collect the scraps left over. Guess what? After everyone had full bellies and contented smiles, the disciples collected more food in leftovers than they'd had to start—twelve full baskets loaded with bread and fish!

Every time I reread this story of the feeding of the five thousand in Scripture, I am struck by three things.

First, Jesus didn't hesitate to issue an impossible challenge to his followers. It never fazed him, didn't bother him in the slightest. You never get the sense that he felt like what he was asking was too much for those he called his own. Sure, it was obviously not an easy task. But was he worried his disciples couldn't handle it? Not for a second. He never said, "Okay, don't feed everybody. How about if you feed only a thousand of them or five hundred? Would that make you feel more comfortable with the challenge?"

Christ didn't shy away from any challenge for the disciples. In fact, in this instance, he even created the challenge for them!

The second thing I notice is that he coached them through the challenge. He didn't say, "Okay, go to it, guys. I'll see you later, when you're done." Nope. He laid out the challenge, then helped them assess their resources (five loaves and two fish) and formulate a strategy for succeeding in meeting the challenge.

The third thing I notice is really just speculation, but I think it's true nonetheless. Jesus Christ wanted his disciples to experience the joy of victory, the sense of accomplishment that comes from facing a difficult task head-on—and kicking its proverbial rear end. Why else would he take advantage of the current situation (thousands of people gathered in one place) and then orchestrate the response to that situation in such a way as to help his disciples rise above the challenge and glorify God in the process?

I think that's so important! You see, we are children of a Father who can—and will—use anything to make us stronger, to lead us into victory over any of life's circumstances. We have a Father in God who, like Jesus did, isn't afraid to take the challenges of your life (and mine)—even serious challenges like the divorce of our parents—and use them to work miracles in response.

Your Father Challenges You to Overcome Your Heritage

That willingness to take on any challenge brings to mind the story of seventy-two-year-old gate-crasher Dion Rich. By the time Super Bowl XXXVI came around (on February 3, 2002), Rich had successfully sneaked into thirty-two straight Super Bowls—and a host of other major events as well!

But sneaking into this Super Bowl in New Orleans, Louisiana, was a much riskier proposition than, say, going ticketless into the World Series or backstage at the Academy Awards. Held just a few months after the tragedy of the 9/11 terrorist attacks on America, security for "the big dance" of football was at a record-setting high. For starters, there were the Secret Service agents, the FBI, FEMA, the National Guard, and U.S. marshals. There were jeeps, humvees, metal detector wands, and even a ten-foot-high chain-link/barbed wire combo fence that surrounded the Louisiana Superdome. In all, the NFL spent seven million dollars on security alone for this one game.

After doing a preliminary check on the security measures, Dion Rich almost gave up on his quest to see a thirty-third straight Super Bowl without buying a ticket. He went through his list of tricks and found them all wanting. Pretending to be a referee wasn't going to cut it this year. Working his way in by sitting in a wheelchair wouldn't do either. Something from his bag of fake press credentials? Nope. It seemed Dion was at an impasse.

Still, a challenge was a challenge, and Mr. Rich wasn't one to give up easily. I'll let *Sports Illustrated* columnist Rick Reilly tell what happened next:

> Wearing a blue blazer and a tie, Albert Einstein's haircut and glasses on the end of his pointy nose, Rich set off to penetrate the most impenetrable fortress in U.S. history.
>
> The fortress lost. Rich was inside in six minutes. I followed him the whole way. It was pure art.[2]

At the first security station, Mr. Rich managed to catch a guard with her head buried in someone else's bag and, quick as lightning, squeezed unnoticed past her and through a one-foot gap between a metal detector and a fence. Next he slid around a guy distracted by his duties of scanning people with a metal detector wand, faded into the crowd to get past a National Guardsman—all this simply to get up to the place where the ticket takers stood in place.

But the ticket takers were no match for Dion. He found a row of doors that locked from the inside and simply waited. Sure enough, it wasn't long before a hurried supervisor came barreling out of one of the doors. Before it could close, Rich was there—literally—with his foot in the door. In a flash, he was inside for the big game.

Reilly reports, "I didn't hear from Dion again until midnight. He called from inside the [St. Louis] Rams postgame party. . . . Thank God he's on our side."[3]

The prospect of taking on the greatest security force in the world was a challenge Dion Rich couldn't resist. And his reward? Bragging rights and free admission to a big game. That's a nice prize, to be sure, but not much in the eternal sense of rewards, is it? Yet, without endorsing his obviously illegal activities, let me say that Mr. Rich shows more courage in his gate-crashing endeavors than most of us do in our lives as children of divorced parents.

Too often you and I look at our experience as children and we know our parents did us no favors by splitting up. We know we've "got issues" as they say in psychological jargon. But instead of viewing our life circumstances as a challenge in which God can work a miracle, we can often be guilty of giving up, of deciding that a fulfilling, Father-focused lifestyle is just too hard. When that happens, we skip the Super Bowl party and end up in our own personal pity parties instead.

What should happen—what *can* happen—is something much greater. Imagine the difference in your life if you took hold of this truth: *God has allowed you to live through the divorce of your parents. Rather than letting this circumstance defeat you for the rest of your life, he now wants to raise that bitter disappointment before you as a challenge, to view it as an opportunity for you to come face-to-face with your broken heritage, and, with your Father's help, to find victory and growth out of the ashes of defeat.*

Friend, that is a truth than can literally change your life—and mine! As William Bennett says, "The question is not whether you will suffer disappointment in life—everyone does—but what it stirs inside you."[4]

Consider the experience of the great artist Michelangelo. During the year of 1494, the young artist sat forgotten and despairing in the city of Florence, Italy. In those days, an artist needed a patron—that is, a wealthy person who sponsored art projects and paid for living and material expenses for the artist, allowing someone like Michelangelo to concentrate solely on his work instead of working at peasant labor to earn money.

For many years, Michelangelo had been fortunate enough to have Duke Lorenzo de'Medici as his patron. It was the duke who had first discovered the sculptor's talent and who invited Michelangelo to live in his palace as part of the duke's household. It was Lorenzo who had become the young man's friend and provided block after block of the finest marble to use for his carvings.

But when the duke passed away, his son Piero ruled in his place. While he let Michelangelo continue to live on the palace grounds, he disdained the artist's work and left him to languish in empty solitude.

Then one wintry day in 1494, as Michelangelo sat by a window watching the snow fall silently on the ground outside, he heard a knock at his door. It was a servant of Piero's come to call the young man to the new duke's presence! Quickly they made their way through the snow-packed lanes back to the main palace. As they walked, the page seemed to grin with perverse pleasure at an unknown joke, and he said, "This is the day you've been waiting for, is it not? To sculpt again for the great Medici family—what could be more wonderful?"

Michelangelo felt hope leap up within him at those words. Moments later he stood before a smirking Piero. The new duke was surrounded by a group of friends and guests, obviously enjoying some sort of party.

"Today we have need of your talent," said Piero in a mocking tone. "You do have great talent, do you not, my friend?"

Turning toward a large window and pointing to the snow-covered countryside, the duke continued, "You will go down to the garden. There you will find all the white marble your heart desires, lying heaped on the ground. I am giving a dinner tonight, and I want my guests to be able to see one of your brilliant statues. Of course, tomorrow morning the sun will do away with all your hard labor. But nothing lasts forever, does it, young maestro?"

Snickers broke out among the crowd of Piero's friends as the reality of the command set in. The new Duke of Medici wanted a sculpture made out of snow—knowing it would melt away to nothing by the next day! Red-hot anger and embarrassment flashed through Michelangelo's body. The duke was deliberately humiliating the artist, simply to make himself look better in the eyes of his friends.

Michelangelo could have replied with anger and insults. He could have walked away and, with his fame and talent, surely would have found a willing patron somewhere else. He could have simply refused and returned to his room on the palace grounds. But he didn't. In the end, he refused to be cowed by a cruel joke at the hands of a piggish man. Instead, he stepped up to the plate and took the challenge head-on.

"I will do your bidding, O great Medici," he responded. Then he turned and went immediately out to the garden. Working in silence in the hardship of cold and loneliness, he determined to overcome. First, he spent long hours simply packing snow, packing snow, and packing more snow until he finally had a large ice-hard block to work with. Finally he was ready, with frozen hands and chilled limbs, to carve.

Caught up in his work, he began to bring exquisite detail out of the block of ice—a head first, then shoulder and a torso, hands and feet, then he went back to the head where the face must be formed, where life must be imitated with detailed precision.

And so he worked, and, at some point in the night, a miracle happened. Out of the hardships of snow and ice and cold and cruel patrons, beauty was formed, a sublime piece of art, created by the hands of the man they called the Pride of Florence.

As Michelangelo stood back to evaluate his work, he heard a gasp. Unknown to him, Duke Piero had stolen silently up beside him and stood gazing at the art form in the snowy garden. Remorse filled his soul as he whispered to his artist, "Snow—not snow! Something this beautiful should never pass away . . ."

From that day forward, Michelangelo's patron became his greatest ally, all because the artist took on the challenge of creating beauty out of hardship, of making a masterpiece out of snow.[5]

Friend, your life has had its share of hardships, there's no denying that. Some would even say that you have had more hardships than most. Now you, like Michelangelo, are being challenged to bring beauty out of sorrow, to create a life that is God's work of art from one that got its start with limited supplies.

Are you up to that challenge? Your Father is, and with his steadying hand to guide and strengthen, you can become more than you ever dreamed you could be.

Your Father Challenges You to Move Forward with Your Life

How do we become that life of beauty the Father challenges us to be? It starts with a commitment to reverse the curse divorce placed in our lives, to let the past stay in the past.

Now curses are curious things. The basic definition of a curse is "an expression wishing evil upon another."[6] Theologian Lawrence Richards says, "A curse binds and limits its object. It brings about diminished circumstances that stand in contrast to the blessing God yearns to provide."[7]

This kind of cursing can sometimes lead to humorous extremes. Although I haven't had a chance to use them yet (thankfully!), I love the wit in many timeless Jewish curses:

> May all your teeth fall out except one—and that should ache you!
> May you grow so rich your widow's second husband never has to worry about making a living!
> May you fall into the outhouse just as a regiment of Ukrainians is finishing a prune stew and twelve barrels of beer![8]

And my personal favorite, overheard from a woman mad at her butcher: "May you have an injury that is not covered by workmen's compensation!"

We can chuckle at the intended humor of these unkind wishes, but the curse of divorce that we experienced, through no fault of our own, is really no laughing matter. However, we can—and should—take a lesson from Jewish malediction and learn to turn our curses into comedy.

Our enemy, the devil, loves it when we tremble in fear and discouragement at his activities. He cannot bear it when we laugh in his face and say like Joseph of ancient days, "You meant to hurt me, but God turned your evil into good" (Gen. 50:20 NCV). How do we do this? First, we must learn to let go of the past, to free ourselves from the power it has over us today.

An anguished woman once wrote to divorce researcher Judith Wallerstein and said, "Dear Dr. Wallerstein, I am a child of divorce. I'm thirty-nine and have a loving husband and two wonderful sons. Yet I go to bed every night worried that when I wake up, they'll be gone. Can you help me?"⁹

That's the kind of power a divorce can hold over people like you and me, disrupting our lives with unneeded agony and unwanted fears. Wallerstein explains:

> Divorce in childhood creates an enduring identity . . . a permanent stamp. . . . Divorce disrupted your life. It came suddenly, unexpectedly, but you realized it was caused voluntarily by the people you loved best and trusted the most. You concluded again, logically and sensibly, that nothing is stable. Anything could happen and change is probably for the worse. Since your parents assured you that things would be better but they weren't you drove your feelings underground even more—where they became more powerful.¹⁰

Now years—decades—later, you find yourself still under the influence of divorce. It's time to let go of the pain and fear of that experience. It's time we took a long hard look at our past, understood it, and by our heavenly Father's grace, defeated it once and for all.

I love the way actress and author Nancy Stafford explains this. She says:

> Sometimes we need to take a look back in order to move into the future that God has planned for us. But we also need to be liberated from the past to live our lives fully and successfully. As devastating as it might have been, the past is just part of our lives. We also have the future, and the present.
>
> "But why did this happen to me?" you may be asking. "Why did I have to go through that?" You may never fully know the answer. But God knows. It was the very thing He used to bring you to where you are right now.¹¹

What Nancy is talking about is retraining—the ability to teach ourselves new habits to free ourselves from the chains of our past hurts. We must retrain ourselves to look beyond the divorce and into our Father's future, to stop asking, "Why me, God?" and start asking, "Now what, God?"

Believe it or not, it reminds me of the circus. Have you ever been inside the big top before the show and been allowed to walk around down by the elephants? The surprise as you stand among these massive beasts is that though each one has the power to crush a house, an elephant in the circus is typically leashed into submission by a modest chain tacked into the ground with an eighteen-inch spike.

Here's the truth. Any of those adult elephants could at any time easily yank that stake right out of the ground and march away to freedom. But none of them do.

I'm told the reason for this lies back in the elephant's childhood. (Is this starting to sound familiar?) When an elephant is a baby, a trainer attaches that selfsame spike and chain to the leg of the animal. A short chain and eighteen-inch stake buried in the ground is more than the baby elephant can overcome. Sure, he tries to yank it out, or she pulls on it over and over again, but each attempt ends in failure for the young elephant. After a time, the little ones quit trying. They simply accept that they can't free themselves from the limiting power of the chain.

As time passes and the scrawny baby elephant grows into a powerful adult, he or she never understands that adulthood brings with it the strength to break free from the limits of childhood. So, day in and day out, circus elephants allow a feckless remnant of their childhood to hold sway over what they can and can't do in the present.[12]

You must understand this. *The overwhelming challenge (your parents' divorce) that bound you as a child need no longer hold any real power in your life!* You are no longer a "baby elephant," but, by your heavenly Father's grace and Spirit, you are a powerful behemoth who can uproot any emotional or spiritual chains that were placed around your heart so many years ago.

Listen to what Judith Wallerstein says about this:

> Try your best to understand that what you felt [about your parents' divorce] was right for a small child to feel. You were an intelligent and loving child who was trying to protect your parents and yourself. You didn't want to burden them with your anger or your fears so you kept them all to yourself. But what was sensible then makes no sense now. *You're an adult who is able to handle all the things that frightened you as a little child. You're no longer helpless in the night.* . . . An adult can cope with feelings that may overwhelm a child.[13]

Do you hear those freeing words? *You're no longer helpless in the night.* To borrow a phrase from humor novelist Douglas Adams, it's been a long, dark teatime of the soul for children like you and me. It's time that we who are now adults flip the switch and flood that place of hurtful memories with the light of God's redeeming, restoring, overcoming power.

Is that easy? Of course not! It's a major challenge the Father has allowed to be placed squarely in the center of your life. Is it a challenge we can overcome? Absolutely. You see, just as God was with the disciples when he told them to feed thousands, he stands beside you and me, coaching, instructing, empowering miracles day by day through the rest of our life—and beyond.

Your Father Challenges You to Live Out His Purpose for You

Dr. Peter Hirsch sheds an interesting light on the meaning of the word *challenge*. "A challenge," he says, "is not the truth. . . . Trace the word back through the Middle English *chalengen* and Old French *chalengier,* all the way to the Latin *calumniari*—and they all turn out to mean 'accuse falsely.' That means a challenge is simply not the truth; it's something that's made up. . . . It is not a lie, but a dream, a hope, an obstacle to overcome, but one that has *not yet* been achieved."[14]

This is the challenge set before us, then—to take the hand of God our Father and step out in faith to reverse the truth about how our parents' divorce can and will affect us.

Sadly, we are too often like the candles in a closet that master storyteller Max Lucado once wrote about.[15] It seems that, as a result of an electrical storm, poor Max's house was plunged into the darkness caused by a power outage. No worries, though, because Max in a flash of foresight had previously stored a number of candles in a closet, ready to be brought out for just such an occasion.

When he reached for the first candle, however, a voice called out sternly, "Hold it right there!"

It was the candle! A red waxy thing that sat on a wooden holder and could produce a strong golden flame. "Don't take me out of here!" it commanded. "Don't take me out of this room. I'm not ready. I need more preparation."

Max was at a loss for words, so the candle continued. "I've decided I need to research this job of light-giving so I won't go out and make a bunch of mistakes. . . . I'm doing some studying. I just finished a book on wind resistance. I'm in the middle of a great series of tapes on wick buildup and conservation—and I'm reading the new best-seller on flame display."

What could Max do? He set down the unprepared candle and reached for another. That's when a chorus of candle voices cried out, "We aren't going either!"

Each one had an excuse for not going. One candle was too busy—he was meditating on the importance of light. Another said he had to get his life together first before he could step out of his comfort zone, and a third said she had to focus on her career as a singer instead. (She sang "This Little Light of Mine" quite nicely, actually.)

So, in the end, poor Max left them all snuffed out in the darkness of the storage closet. They let their excuses prevent them from fulfilling their purpose in life.

Friend, what are the excuses you make for refusing God's challenge? Don't you realize those excuses are keeping you from living out your Father's fulfilling purpose for your life? Your parents' divorce wasn't the end of your life; it was a stepping-stone that God wants to use to make you stronger, faster, brighter in your world. Does that mean your life will be easy? Of course not. But it does mean difficulty doesn't have to be something you fear or let overcome you.

Steven Curtis Chapman is probably one of my favorite Christian singers of all time. Apparently a lot of people agree with me on that, because this guy has managed to sell millions and millions of records and taken home dozens of awards in the process as well. But I digress.

On his 2001 album *Declaration,* the man they affectionately call SC^2 included a song called "Bring It On." The first time I heard this song, I turned to my wife and said, "I know this song."

Now, let me make it clear. I had never heard the song before, nor did I memorize its lyrics or tune ahead of time. But as Steven sang out the words of pain and commitment, my spirit identified with his and with the sentiment of the lyrics. I *knew* this song, and I'm betting you do too.

In "Bring It On," SC^2 begins by telling that he hasn't come looking for trouble, and he doesn't care to fight for no reason. But then his voice gets determined and you can nearly feel the stiffening of his spine, and he vows that in spite of that, he's not going to run and hide if trouble comes looking for him.

Then, explaining how challenges in life can serve to strengthen us, he fairly shouts the words, *"Bring it on! Let the trouble come, let the hard rain fall, let it make me strong. Bring it on . . ."*[16]

It's a great song. But what's even more powerful is to hear Steven tell the story behind it. Believe it or not, he first had the idea for "Bring It On" while attending a high school football game. In fact he even called his own voice mail and left himself a message humming the tune so he wouldn't forget it!

A few months later, he picked it back up again and began working on the lyrics and fleshing out the music for his new album. At that point, he was working with an abstract, inspiring concept. Then he received a startling phone call. I'll let him tell what happened next:

> The day I was working on one of the verses [for "Bring It On"] my mom called me and told me she had been diagnosed with cancer. I really debated at that point whether to finish the song. I thought that's a bold statement. I thought it might even be stupid to make that statement. I knew what I meant by it but was that just asking for trouble? . . . I really wrestled with this song. I decided to finish it and put it on the record. . . . I can honestly say that I think it's something that is truth. I need to be able to say it and need to say, "God, if it's gonna bring me closer to You and be a part of Your hand at work in my life, then let it come, bring it on."[17]

When Steven Curtis Chapman made the decision to record and publish "Bring It On," he really made a decision to put his faith on the line. He, in a few simple words, affirmed the truth that life is filled with challenges, but God always has a purpose for his children. What it boiled down to is this: SC^2 determined to trust God's purpose and power in his life *no matter what.*

Now, you and I stand at the same crossroads that Steven did. We may or may not be facing cancer, but we are facing the aftereffects of our past. Will we determine to press on, to march fearlessly into the unknown future, holding tightly to our Father's guiding hand?

Can we look the devil square in the eye and say, "Bring it on! Sure you hurt me when you nudged my parents toward divorce, but is that the best you can do? 'Cause it ain't enough. Nothing is. No matter what you do, no matter what schemes you try, no matter what kind of pain you inflict, you can never—ever—cause more hurt than my Father can heal. So is that all you got? You ain't nothing, pal, and you dress funny too. You want a piece of me? Then bring it on, 'cause you have to face more than just me. You have to go up against God himself, and he will kick your tail from here to eternity."

Can I be honest for a moment? I'm not there quite yet, but I want to be. And I believe that, with my Father fighting beside me, sooner or later I will overcome every challenge the enemy has thrown or will throw at me. And I believe you can too.

So let me close this chapter with more than just a little trash talk for Satan. Let me end this one with God doing the trash talking—with the promises he has made to you and me—and with a hearty "amen, Father! Make it so!"

> And we know that God causes all things to work together for good to those who love God, to those who are called according to His purpose.
>
> Romans 8:28 NASB

> Have I not commanded you? Be strong and courageous. Do not be terrified; do not be discouraged, for the LORD your God will be with you wherever you go.
>
> Joshua 1:9

> He gives strength to the weary and increases the power of the weak. Even youths grow tired and weary, and young men stumble and fall; but those who hope in the LORD will renew

their strength. They will soar on wings like eagles; they will run and not grow weary, they will walk and not be faint.

Isaiah 40:29–31

The righteous face many troubles, but the LORD rescues them from each and every one.

Psalm 34:19 NLT

[Jesus said], "I have told you all this so that you may have peace in me. Here on earth you will have many trials and sorrows. But take heart, because I have overcome the world."

John 16:33 NLT

Something to Think About . . .

Use the following questions either by yourself or with a group to process what you've learned in this chapter.

- Why do you suppose God allows his children to face very real, very painful challenges in life?
- In what ways have you seen God bring beauty out of the hardship of your parents' divorce?
- What excuses do you make for putting off the fulfilling life that your Father can infuse in you?
- What would it take for you to be able to say "bring it on" to any challenge that may come your way in this life? What can you do this week to help you get to that point?

Something to Do

Go to a sporting event. As you watch the action, try to identify the challenges the athletes have to overcome to be victorious. Afterward, make a list of the five biggest challenges you feel you have to face to live victoriously over the hurt of your past. Then spend some time in prayer, asking your Father for specific guidance and power to help you face—and overcome—the challenges you listed.

9

A Father Who Empowers You

I love to hear stories about Scottish Olympian Eric Liddell. Born the son of missionary parents in China, he grew up in his parents' home country of Scotland, at a school for missionary children.

Liddell is probably most famous for his unwillingness, in 1924, to run in an Olympic race scheduled on a Sunday—a day he felt was intended strictly for rest. At first ridiculed by the press for refusing to run, he won the world's admiration the next day by running in—and setting a world record for—the 400-meter race for which he'd barely trained. His gold medal in that event made him an icon in Olympic history.

Still, I want to bring your attention to two other stories from Eric Liddell's life—one that happened before the 1924 Olympics and one that happened after.

In 1923 Eric was a student at Edinburgh University, where he was studying science and also participating in the school's athletic events. His natural speed in track soon had people talking about a possible Olympic bid for the twenty-one-year-old Scot.

On this particular day, he lined up to run yet another race, hoping to win (of course). Before the competition, the courteous young man had been the brunt of a few guffaws from the crowd because he had taken a moment to shake the hands of all his rivals, wishing them a good race. But now he was all business, ready to explode from the start on his way to yet another victory.

And that's just what he did, blowing out of his stance at the sound of the starter's pistol and taking three long strides toward the finish line. Just then the runner next to him, a man named Gillies, tripped and stumbled, slamming into Eric and inadvertently forcing him off the track. In the grass, Liddell came to a dejected halt, certain he'd been disqualified from the event. Then he saw the race officials waving him on!

Since he'd been pushed off the track through no fault of his own, he was allowed to continue in the race—but by now the other runners were a good twenty yards ahead and going at full speed too. Still, the young Scotsman bolted back onto the track, determined to finish the race even if it was in last place.

Much to the surprise of the crowd, Eric quickly made up space between him and the other runners, and by the time they rounded the corner for the home stretch, he was in fourth place! Gillies, the runner who had stumbled, had recovered enough to be in first place—but Eric was gaining.

His lungs practically screamed for oxygen as his body threatened to buckle under the intense pace of this battle for first place. But Eric, refusing to quit, kept his arms and legs pumping. He passed the third-place runner, then the second, but now the finish line loomed close and Gillies was still ahead. Then, with an unexpected surge, he pushed past the front-runner and crossed the tape two full yards ahead of the pack. He had done the impossible—been knocked out of the race, come to a full stop, and still managed to reenter the race and win!

The stadium cascaded with cheers and a newspaper reporter came rushing over to the exhausted Scotsman. "How did you manage to win such an impossible race?" the reporter asked.

Eric smiled and shook his head, then said, "The first half I ran as fast as I could. The second half I ran faster with God's help!"

God's empowering presence was all over Eric Liddell's life—even in something as trivial as running a track-and-field race. It's a good thing too, because two decades later he would need his Father's power to finish a much more difficult race.

After he won the gold in the 1924 Olympics, many expected Eric Liddell to "cash in" on his newfound fame and status as an athletic hero. He did just the opposite, thrusting himself into obscurity to go to China as a missionary teacher to the people there. In the 1940s World War II raged, and Eric became one of its victims.

As an outsider in China, he became a target of the Chinese Communist government. They arrested the missionary and interned him in a harsh prison camp for foreigners. While there, he developed a brain tumor, adding to his suffering.

Even though he was ill, imprisoned, and living in degrading conditions, Eric Liddell still experienced the empowering presence of God. As days turned to weeks, and weeks to years, he continued to serve others in the camp with grace and encouragement, challenging everyone to be a winner for the cause of Christ.

In 1944, just months before the end of the war, Eric Liddell finished the race God had set before him when the tumor in his brain finally took his life. When he crossed that finish line, he traded his gold medal for streets of gold, his humble sufferings for a crown of glory, the power of God's grace for the joy of God's grasp as he fell into his Father's arms in his eternal home, heaven.[1]

Why do I tell you these two stories about this remarkable man? It is to remind you that Eric Liddell's Father is also your Father and to encourage you with the news that the same God who empowered the Scotsman to win a race, to serve as a missionary, to endure the hardships of prison camp, and to face death from an incurable illness is the same Father today that he was back then. You have a Father who can—and will—empower you to face down anything that has been or will be in your life.

Your Father Empowers You with His Vision *for* You

Let me tell you about the opening day at Walt Disney World in Florida. Walt Disney had passed away before the grand park could open, and his son attended the opening festivities in his place. A reporter paused to give the young man his condolences.

Motioning toward the magnificent spectacle that surrounded them, he said, "It's too bad Walt didn't live to see this."

Walt's son just smiled and said, "He did. That's why you're looking at it now."[2]

What a great example of the power of vision in a person's life! Walt Disney had "seen" the potential, the possibilities, the what-might-be that eluded the minds of his contemporaries. As a result, he created a lasting legacy of entertainment known the world over.

Now here's the really good news: Your Father's vision for you extends farther than Walt Disney could ever imagine, and by focusing on God's vision, you open the doorway for him to empower your life and unlock your undiscovered potential.

Scripture tells us, "Where there is no vision, the people perish" (Prov. 29:18 KJV). And it also reveals that "No eye has seen, no ear has heard, no mind has conceived what God has prepared for those who love him" (1 Cor. 2:9).

Now please understand this. When your parents divorced, God's vision for you was never that you should live a life emotionally crippled or spiritually helpless as a result. When you felt the sorrow of loneliness into adulthood, it was not God's vision for you to spend the rest of your life in that deep, dark valley.

Your Father's vision for you goes so far beyond that weak little image that it's indescribable. My words that attempt to describe it can, of necessity, be only inarticulate and crude representations of God's awesome vision for your life potential.

You see, God's vision for you stretches through yesterday, weaves into today, extends into tomorrow, and guarantees eternity. It is a vision for freedom, for health, and for life, all found within the hands and heart of Jesus Christ.

Perhaps the best way to illustrate this is to tell another story. This one is about Henry Brown. Henry lived during the 1800s and was a slave in pre–Civil War America. Despite his servile circumstances, Mr. Brown had a vision for what his life could be; in his mind's eye he could see his heart's greatest desire—freedom.

The trouble was that freedom for Henry Brown lay far away in Philadelphia, and he lived and worked on a plantation in Virginia. So he began to pray, daily, constantly for God's hand to bring about his freedom.

One day during prayer, Henry felt as though God himself spoke words into his mind: "Go and get a box, and put yourself in it."

Mr. Brown later recorded, "I pondered these words over in my mind. 'Get a box?' thought I. 'What can this mean?' But

. . . I determined to put into practice this direction, as I considered it, from my heavenly Father."

So on his next trip to the train station, the slave took a few moments to study the size and style of boxes used for shipping. Soon the vision came clear into his mind. Henry Brown would mail himself to freedom!

This course of action was inherently dangerous, but the slave refused to lose sight of the vision at the end of his hardship—freedom. Over the next weeks he enlisted a friend sympathetic to his cause to build him a wooden box, three feet by two feet and with only three small airholes in it, that could be used for shipping. He corresponded with abolitionist friends in Philadelphia and soon it was decided. Henry would enter into this tiny prison and have himself shipped to Philadelphia where his abolitionist colleagues promised to receive him and ferry him to final freedom.

On the fateful day, Henry Brown had more than misgivings—he was scared to death! He later reported, "I laid me down in my darkened home of three feet by two, and like one about to be guillotined, resigned myself to my fate."

His fears were not unfounded. Although the box was clearly marked "This Side Up," it was advice handlers routinely ignored. Said Henry, "I was put aboard a steamboat, *and placed on my head.* In this dreadful position, I remained . . . when I began to feel of my eyes and head and found to my dismay, that my eyes were almost swollen out of their sockets, and the veins on my temple seemed ready to burst."

Half an hour later, Henry couldn't move his hands and truly expected to die. Yet he recalled later, "I made no noise, however, determining to obtain *victory or death,* but endured the terrible pain, as well as I could, sustained under the whole by the thoughts of sweet liberty."

Even in the face of seemingly unbearable pain and death, the vision of freedom was so strong in this man's life that *he didn't make a sound* because that would have betrayed his purpose and extinguished his vision. By God's grace, after he had spent two hours upside down, the handlers stopped for a break and turned Henry's box over so they could rest against it.

For the rest of the long journey, besides the obvious discomfort of being smashed inside a small box with little oxygen and no food, Henry Brown endured being tossed onto his head within the box, near dislocation of his neck, intense heat, exhaustion, and a threat of being left behind at one point. Yet in the end, his box was delivered to Philadelphia, where several friends had gathered to receive him. In all honesty, they expected to find him dead and actually delayed opening the box because of that fear!

When they finally ripped open Henry's box—a process he described as "opening my grave"—the man stood, then promptly fainted. But when he awoke, he was a slave no longer; Henry "Box" Brown was free.[3]

Friend, the aftereffects of growing up as a child of divorce threaten to leave you and me as slaves to our past, shackled, burdened, emotionally chained in service to the hurt we once endured. I won't lie to you. This life we now live is hard. It still hurts, and its pain can hasten death.

But that is not God's vision for you and me.

God's empowering vision for you is freedom, freedom from the negative influences of your childhood and even from your present experience, freedom from your own failings that hinder you each day, freedom to slip out of the shackles of anger and bitterness that threaten to hold onto your life, freedom to break the cursing legacy of divorce, to live out your own fulfilling marriage, and pass a new legacy on to your own children.

Scripture promises freedom:

[Jesus said,] "And you will know the truth, and the truth will make you free."

John 8:33 NASB

151

So now, those who are in Christ Jesus are not judged guilty. Through Christ Jesus the law of the Spirit that brings life made me free from the law that brings sin and death.

Romans 8:1–2 NCV

Now the Lord is the Spirit, and where the Spirit of the Lord is, there is freedom.

2 Corinthians 3:17

We have freedom now, because Christ made us free. So stand strong. Do not change and go back into the slavery of the law.

Galatians 5:1 NCV

[Jesus said,] "The Spirit of the Lord is on me, because he has anointed me to preach good news to the poor. *He has sent me to proclaim freedom for the prisoners* and recovery of sight for the blind, to release the oppressed, to proclaim the year of the Lord's favor."

Luke 4:18–19; italics mine

Friend, this is your Father's vision for you, and when you embrace that vision and make it your own, it will empower you to accomplish more than you ever could think or imagine!

Still, it's sometimes hard to maintain faith in this powerful vision God has for you and me; in fact in our own strength it's impossible. Thank goodness we don't have to rely on ourselves to accomplish God's vision for us! We have a great Helper, an awesome Enabler who empowers us moment by moment, day by day—the Holy Spirit of God, present in every iota of our being, empowering us to overcome.

Your Father Empowers You with His Holy Spirit *in* You

Theologian J. B. Phillips once said, "Every time we say, 'I believe in the Holy Spirit,' we mean that we believe that there is a living God able and willing to enter human personality and change it."[4]

You see, the greatest promise that Jesus Christ ever gave to us was this one regarding the Holy Spirit: "I will ask the Father, and *He will give you another Helper to be with you forever,* even the Spirit of truth. . . . You know Him, for *He dwells with you and will be in you.* I will not leave you as orphans; I will come to you" (John 14:16–18 ESV; italics mine).

As I mentioned back in chapter 7, the Greek word used to reference the Holy Spirit in this passage is *parakletos*—the root we use for our English word *paraclete,* which literally means "one who is called alongside." Author Gordon Dalbey discovered an interesting history behind the meaning of this word.

"Greek soldiers went into battle in pairs," he reports, "so when the enemy attacked, they could draw together back-to-back, covering each other's blind side. One's battle partner was the Paraclete. Our Lord does not send us to fight the good fight alone. The Holy Spirit is our battle partner who covers our blind side and fights for our well being."[5]

What an encouragement that is for people like you and me! Our lives are not easy—no life is, really. Yet through it all we are never left alone. We have a champion, a Paraclete who enters the battle with us, who often does the battle for us. And he is no weak comrade at arms; in fact he is not capable of defeat. Though he may allow the enemy's darts and arrows to prick us, he will never allow the enemy to overcome us. And it is by his power that we become empowered to face fear, to face opposition, to face anger and bitterness and pain and anything else the devil may try to throw our way.

Here is what the apostle Paul said about this: "For God has not given us a spirit of fear, *but of power* and of love and of a sound mind" (2 Tim. 1:7 NKJV; italics mine). And let us remember to take to heart Jesus' promise: "But *you will receive power* when the Holy Spirit comes on you" (Acts 1:8; italics mine).

This is one of the "fringe benefits" of being adopted into the family of God. We as God's children are entitled to receive the great gift of God's own Spirit to dwell within— and empower—us without limit, without end.

I love the way renowned nineteenth-century preacher Dwight Moody viewed this situation. "God commands us to be filled with the Spirit," he said, "and if we are not filled, it is because we are living beneath our privileges!"[6]

Sometimes the Holy Spirit empowers us from within to bring about his purpose in our lives. That was the case with young Christian singer Nikki Leonti.

By the time she was seventeen years old, Nikki had accomplished what many older musicians merely dream of. This talented vocalist had already released her debut album, *Shelter Me*—a CD that immediately rode up the charts to a slot in *CCM Update's* top five Christian albums and earned a place in the top twelve on *Billboard* magazine's prestigious charts. She had also toured the nation, treating fans all over to her infectious brand of pop music.

If you watched how confidently Nikki took the stage for a show, you'd think this talented teen had everything going for her—fame, a bright future, and little to fear. What you might not notice is the fact that Nikki often suffered through bouts of stage fright.

Oh, she wasn't frightened of singing, of course. Nikki loved to sing. That came easily. But a performer is also expected to *talk,* to share a bit of her life with the audience—that's where Nikki had trouble.

"I had a problem talking when I sang or did a concert," she admits. "I always knew what I wanted and needed to say to people, but I had a fear that they would think I sounded juvenile. I also wanted the courage to talk about past circumstances, such as [when] my six-year-old brother died of cancer. . . . I wanted to share about that but I never knew how to word it."

So for concert after concert, Nikki would sail through her songs with ease, then stumble over her words when it came time to speak. She knew something had to be done— and she knew who could help.

Nikki turned to the One who created her mouth, who blessed her with the talent to sing. She prayed, asking Jesus to empower her, to give her courage to share and wisdom to speak the words that others needed to hear. She felt certain that in each audience there might be at least one person who would be helped by hearing how Jesus had brought her through trials and hard times in her young life. So she prayed for God's Holy Spirit to help her overcome her stage fright, for God to use her speaking to minister to those who came to hear her sing.

One night in March of 1998, Nikki stood where she often did, onstage. Little did she know that in the audience that day a young man was hurting. His brother was fighting a losing battle against cancer. He felt so helpless, so discouraged with the knowledge that his brother would soon be gone, but he didn't know what to do about it.

Neither Nikki nor the young man could have guessed that each one had gone through the same agony. But in between songs, Nikki felt God's Spirit flowing through her and, with new courage, shared a bit of her testimony with the audience. She told of the despair she felt when her brother passed away and how Christ had brought her through that time.

The young man sat in rapt attention, suddenly realizing he was not alone. After the concert, he sought Nikki out and told her of his own experience. Then the two young people prayed together, thanking God that he had brought them to this place at this time and asking God for strength and healing in the days to come.

Afterward, Nikki thought about how things might have been different if God's empowering Holy Spirit hadn't given her the courage to speak about her life. That young man might have walked away never knowing that Jesus could indeed carry him through this time of trouble.

Today Nikki reports that the Holy Spirit continues to answer her prayer for courage. She rarely struggles with stage fright anymore, saying, "Now I share [my] testimony at every concert. And at least one person in the audience will be going through the same thing. I've learned now to open up and share what the Lord is leading me to say."[7]

Sometimes, God's Holy Spirit empowers us by fighting the spiritual battles that go on outside of ourselves. Such was the case with R&B/gospel singer Debbie Winans.

"My mom always taught us, 'If you ever get in trouble, call on Jesus,'" says Debbie. "I used to think, *Yeah, yeah, all right,*" dismissing her mother's advice as irrelevant.

Then one day the young woman was walking home from school, walking down the street of her family's Detroit neighborhood when she was violently mugged. A man jumped out in front of her, demanding her valuables. Debbie recalls, "He went to grab at a necklace I had on and grabbed so hard that he knocked me to the ground. Then he straddled on top of me with his legs and bent down. I thought, *Oh my God, I'm about to be raped and killed, and there's no one around!*"

Fear threatened to paralyze the young woman, when the Spirit of God miraculously brought her mother's instruction back to her mind. *If you ever get in trouble, call on Jesus.*

"I was looking around," Debbie continues. "Where'd all the cars go? Under my breath I kept saying, 'Jesus, Jesus, Jesus . . .' He said, *'What'd you say?'* and I said, 'Jesus.' He said, *'Don't say that!'* I said 'Oh, Jesus . . . the blood of Jesus!' and the man got up and ran! He was so mad at me for calling that name, but he ran. . . . I have seven brothers, but no one was home. They all could have beat [that man] up, but they weren't there. So I realized, *Jesus did it. I called His name and the man ran.*"[8]

That's the kind of power God's Holy Spirit wields in this world of ours—a power that can fight the battles within and win the battles without. And often the Holy Spirit empowers us not only with strength and courage but with his wisdom as well.

There is a story of two young princes—just boys, really—who occupied the throne of Russia. The two child-czars were often forced to make very difficult judgments about matters of state and in resolving disputes brought before them by the people. Yet time and time again the children would listen to the cases and then deliver a sound, wise judgment.

People marveled at the czars' wisdom and skill in handling the tough decisions of their rule together . . . until one day it was discovered that each time the boys sat in judgment, they never sat alone. Hidden behind a curtain where she could whisper into her brothers' ears was Princess Sophia. It was she who stood always nearby and she who empowered the boys to rule justly by giving them wise advice from behind the curtain.[9]

This is often how the Holy Spirit empowers you and me to govern our past, present, and future as well. He stands always nearby, whispering God's wisdom into the "ears" of our heart and mind, directing us ever forward toward the great eternal victory that God has planned for us, his children.

Your Father Empowers You with His Grace *toward* You

Wrapped up in the powerful presence of our Father's Holy Spirit is something you and I desperately need—God's empowering grace in our lives. Rev. Billy Graham explains why this is so important. He says, "The grace of God has been tested in the crucible of human experience, and has been found more than an equal for the problems and sins of humanity."[10]

Make no mistake. Divorce is a sin and one of the major problems of modern humanity. But it is no unconquerable force in our lives. The grace of God transcends that experience and, if we allow it, will lift us above our past as well.

And the fact is we ourselves are prone to sin and failure, just like our parents were. In truth, any weakness we've seen—and felt the fallout from—in our parents (or anyone else) is one of which we also can be guilty. The apostle Paul made that clear when he stated in no uncertain terms, "None is righteous, no not one" (Rom. 3:10 ESV).

What a joyful relief to know that God's lifesaving grace will intervene on our behalf in any and all of these situations! We have in our Father a loyal lover of our souls who will always extend to us the favor of his fatherhood. Yes, he may discipline us; yes, he will allow us to endure difficulty; but he will never remove his grace, forgiveness, and mercy from us—no matter what.

I love the way theologian Don Campbell explains this:

> Grace [is] God's unmerited favor in the giving of His Son, through whom salvation is offered to all. . . . Grace provides acceptance with God (Rom. 3:24), gives enablement to live for God (Col. 1:29; Titus 2:11–12), establishes the believer in a new position (1 Peter 2:9), and bestows on

the saved every spiritual blessing for this life and the life
to come (Eph. 1:3–14).[11]

It's sad that, even though we have experienced this transforming power of grace ourselves, we Christians are often
more familiar with what Philip Yancey calls "the black hole
of 'ungrace.'"[12] "Oddly," Yancey says, "I sometimes find a
shortage of grace within the church, an institution founded
to proclaim, in Paul's phrase, 'the gospel of God's grace.'"[13]

I encountered what Yancey speaks of just this week. As a
columnist for a prominent Christian magazine, I often get
e-mail in response to what I've written. Recently I wrote
about an entertainment product that is popular among some
Christians and disliked by others. In my column I listed both
sides of the argument and recommended the reader make
the final decision. I also recommended a book by scholar
and novelist C. S. Lewis as an additional resource.

One of my readers, a person named John, promptly sent
me this note:

> [You] can't possibly know Jesus as lord [sic]. And C. S. Lewis
> is no different. . . . You won't make Heaven going down the
> road you are traveling. I pray you will repent.
> JESUS loves YOU.
> John

Another reader, a man named Stan, e-mailed this to me:

> Did God send you a memo that He changed His mind about
> witchcraft and I did not get it? . . . If you know how to use a
> commentary, you can see that there are more [Bible verses]
> against witchcraft then [sic] abortion. . . . I thought [maga-
> zine name] was Christian. I guess I was wrong.
> Stan

I can't even count the number of times my Christian brothers and sisters have sent me mail like this—or how many

have summarily condemned me straight to hell because of something I have written. (Apparently C. S. Lewis is already there too!) If I allowed the "ungrace" of these frequent letters to cloud from my vision the true power of God's grace in my life, I'd never write another word again! But ungrace should never rule the life of one of God's children—you and me included.

You see, ungrace isn't limited to unkind letters from spiritual family members; it reigns in just about every area of life, from the supermarket checkout to the hospital room to the battlefields of war to the emotional (and sometimes physical) combat zone in our living rooms. Yet, as God's priceless heirs, we do not have to succumb to the crushing power of ungrace in our lives. No matter the circumstance, no matter the pain, no matter the guilt or retribution we endure, our Father's grace will still flow daily, hourly, empowering us to persevere and overcome.

At the risk of angering my friend John again, I think C. S. Lewis once described this beautifully. He said:

> If and when horror turns up you will then be given Grace to help you. I don't think one is usually given it in advance. "Give us our daily bread" (not an annuity for life) applies to spiritual gifts too; the little *daily* support for the *daily* trial. Life has to be taken day by day and hour by hour.[14]

And this is another wonderful thing about the way God's grace can empower your life. It is always sufficient for the day's troubles and failures. It's like a story Charles Spurgeon once told of a fortune left to a poor minister in England.

It seems a wealthy benefactor passed away and in his will left one hundred pounds for the poor minister, with instructions that his friend, a Mr. Rowland Hill, dispense the money as he saw fit. As Mr. Hill prepared to forward the wealth to the minister, he realized the large sum would probably be overwhelming for the man. So, instead of sending it all, he sent a five-pound note in an envelope, with a note attached that said, "More to follow."

A few days later, he sent another five pounds, again with a note that said, "More to follow." And again, the same thing a few days after that. Before long, the minister found all his needs met, five pounds at a time, always joyfully anticipating the promise that there was "more to follow."

I love the way Spurgeon finishes telling this story, so I'll let him do the honors here:

> Every blessing that comes from God is sent with the self-same message: "And more to follow." "I forgive you your sins, but there's more to follow." "I justify you in the righteousness of Christ, but there's more to follow." "I educate you for Heaven, but there's more to follow." "I give you grace upon grace, but there's more to follow." "I have helped you even to old age, but there's still more to follow." "I will uphold you in the hour of death, and as you are passing into the world of spirits, my mercy shall still continue with you, and when you land in the world to come there shall still be *more to follow.*"[15]

If you are like me, sometimes you feel all used up, beaten and bruised by the circumstances of your world. Perhaps you lie down at night and sigh, feeling empty and like you have nothing left to fight the frustrations and heartaches and failures that are sure to come tomorrow. In those sad, silent moments, remember that God's empowering grace is a never-ending flow in your life and even if you find yourself facing hardship before the sun rises, you can cry out for mercy and be confident that God will answer, "Take heart, my child, there's still more grace to follow."

Let me close this chapter with a promise and a prayer. First is the promise, spoken by the Rev. Billy Graham. He says:

> There is no limit to God.
> There is no limit to His wisdom.

There is no limit to His power.
There is no limit to His love.
There is no limit to His mercy.[16]

When it feels as though God's empowering presence is wearing thin in your life, remember that promise, and let it return you to God's vision for you, to your Father's Holy Spirit within you, and to the experience of his grace toward you.

And now, the prayer, one first spoken by Robert Louis Stevenson. May it be on my lips and yours as we learn to trust in the power of our heavenly Father in our lives:

[God,] give us grace and strength
to forbear and
to persevere.
Give us courage
and gaiety
and the quiet mind.
Spare to us our friends,
Soften to us our enemies.[17]

Amen!

Something to Think About . . .

Use the following questions either by yourself or with a group to process what you've learned in this chapter.

- When have you felt, without a doubt, God's empowering presence in your life? How did you respond to it?
- When are you most likely to feel that God's power is absent from your life? What's the best response in that situation?

- What keeps you from accessing the power and presence of the Holy Spirit in your life? What can you do about it?
- How can God's empowering grace help you overcome any "ungrace" you might encounter this week?

Something to Do

Give yourself a visual demonstration of the need for God's power in your life.

In a darkened room, turn on a flashlight. Then turn it off and remove the batteries, and try to get the flashlight to light the room again. (Of course it won't work without the light-giving power of the batteries!) Pause to thank God for sending his Holy Spirit to be the "power source" in your life, just as a battery is a power source for a flashlight.

Before you're done, place a battery from the flashlight in your purse or pocket and carry it around for a day as a constant reminder of God's empowering presence in your life.

10

A Father Who Enjoys You—
and Wants You to Enjoy Him

Sometimes a little misunderstanding can be a humorous, generally harmless thing. Take the case of a duo of robbers who determined to rob a bank in India. They crashed through the door and, guns raised ominously, demanded cash from the bank manager. He refused, however, saying he didn't have any money.

That's when the robbers realized they'd made a mistake. The "bank" they'd targeted was actually an organ transplant center—an "eye bank" that medical officials used for eye surgeries.

There is a happy ending to this tale of mistaken identity. Before the would-be robbers left, the eye bank manager convinced them to sign pledges promising to donate their own eyes to medicine after they died![1]

Or take the example of a few nameless missionaries to the Igbo people of Nigeria in the 1800s. It seems these well-meaning folk wanted to share with their African converts the pleasures of singing praise and thanksgiving to God. So they undertook the translation of several hymns from their homeland into the language of their flock and proceeded to teach the people these well-loved, God-honoring songs.

The only trouble was that the missionaries misunderstood the tonal quality of the Igbo people's language. They didn't realize that the same word spoken in a higher or lower pitch became an altogether different word to their hearers. The result? For many years—until the mistake was finally understood—the missionaries had their congregants singing classic hymns like, "God's Pig, Which Is Never Shared" and "There Is No Egg on the Bicycle"![2]

Or take the many examples of misused English and typographical errors that pop up in the weekly bulletins of churches around the world. A few of my favorites:

- Low Self-Esteem Support Group will meet Thursday at 7 P.M. Please use the back door.
- The pastor will preach his farewell message, after which the choir will sing, "Break Forth in Joy."
- Due to the Rector's illness, Wednesday's healing services will be discontinued until further notice.
- The eighth-graders will be presenting Shakespeare's *Hamlet* in the church basement on Friday at 7 P.M. The congregation is invited to attend this tragedy.
- The concert held in Fellowship Hall was a great success. Special thanks are due to the minister's daughter who labored the whole evening at the piano which, as usual, fell upon her.
- Twenty members were present at the meeting held at the home of Mrs. Marsha Crutchfield last evening. Mrs. Crutchfield and Mrs. Rankin sang a duet, "The Lord Knows Why."
- A songfest was hell at the Methodist church Wednesday.

165

- The pastor is on vacation this week. Massages can be given to the church secretary.[3]

Yes, sometimes we can get a good laugh out of a false impression or two. But when we have misunderstandings about our Father in heaven, those delusions are deadly to the soul. Sadly, we as children of divorce can be especially susceptible, making those kinds of mistakes about God—and they can affect us for a lifetime.

Your Father Loves You *and* Likes You

One of the greatest fallacies many of us have about God is in regard to his nature. You see, it's easy for us to ascribe to God all the "sharp edges" of his personality:

God is righteous (and we are not)!
God is holy (and we are not)!
God hates sin (and we are sinners)!

And the list goes on. But in discovering these truths, we often get an unspoken impression that, yes, God is our Father but he'd really rather not have to bother with us personally. After all, haven't we failed him time and again, turned our back on him and his standards for life, acted in ways that embarrass his holy family of faith?

The idea—whether conscious or unconscious—that God does not enjoy being with you is a lie whispered straight from the lips of Satan. Let me illustrate it this way. There was a woman, so the story goes, who owned a beautiful—and exceptionally large—diamond ring. Everywhere she went, the diamond elicited stares and comments of admiration.

One day the woman was on an airplane flight headed from Miami to Los Angeles. After a while the lady seated next to her couldn't help but comment. "Excuse me," she said, "I just have to say that is probably the loveliest diamond ring I've ever seen."

"Thank you," replied the first woman. "It's forty carats."

"Forty carats!" gushed the lady. "I never heard of one so big!"

"I know," said the ring bearer. "It even has a name."

"A name? How wonderful! What is it?"

"The Plotnik diamond. And believe me, it's not so wonderful," sighed the first woman. "It comes with a curse. A terrible curse!"

The seatmate was silent for a bit, but in the end couldn't contain her curiosity. "Tell me," she whispered confidentially, "what's the terrible curse that goes with the diamond?"

In hushed tones, the owner of the ring replied, "*Mister* Plotnik!"[4]

We may chuckle at this amusing story, but too often Mrs. Plotnik's is the same kind of attitude we attribute to God! Subconsciously, we believe that we must be the "curse" that God has to endure because of Jesus' death and resurrection. He loves the "jewel" found in Christ and simply endures us as the unpleasant by-product of Jesus' saving work.

How do I know you think this? Because this type of attitude, while often unspoken, is a typical misperception of people who struggle with issues of low self-esteem. You and I were devalued when our parents split up—and we knew it. We knew back then that our love and our presence weren't enough to keep Dad or Mom around the house. Then we endured the harsh realities of a single-parent home where the need for income crowded out our needs for time with our parents and where Dad (or Mom) had to welcome us only on the weekends and for a week or two during the summer. We became secondary in the lives of both of our parents, something they had to "work in" as they had time. And so, despite the words we heard from them, we took to heart the message of their actions: "I'm not good enough. I'm not pretty enough. I'm not smart enough. I'm not valuable, even to my parents."

Now, decades later, we have taken those misconceptions about ourselves and our parents and attached them to God, our heavenly Father. Thus we subconsciously regard ourselves to some degree as the terrible curse of the Plotnik diamond!

And that, my friend, is why I had to write this last chapter in this book for you, to be at least one voice in your life that will tell you the truth. God does *not* view you or your relationship with him as a burden or a curse; each time his eye falls on you, it makes him smile. Your Father *enjoys* being with you—so much so that he will (and has!) moved heaven and earth just so you two can spend time together.

After many years of thinking it through, I finally came to the conclusion that my earthly father did in fact love me. No, he never told me in so many words that he did, but I believe that he did, in his own way. As a father myself, I find it hard to believe that any man could not have feelings of tenderness toward a child that he helped to create. What I never really knew, though, was whether or not my father *liked* me.

He never called to see if I wanted to "just hang out" with him. He never invited me to a play or a baseball game or a movie. He never sat up chatting with me into the wee hours of the night. He never welcomed me with a hug or even a friendly punch on the arm. From my perspective he always seemed distant and relieved when my time with him was done. Perhaps I'm mistaken in my perception, but like it or not, that's the way his actions and his words spoke to me.

Did my father like me? Did he enjoy seeing and spending time with me? Did he eagerly await the days when we would be reunited? Honestly, I don't think so. His divorce from my mother carried such bitterness and acrimony that I fear it influenced his response to all his children. Too often my shadow in his doorway meant another argument with my mother or an unexpected financial expense that he would be forced to bear, and that in turn developed within him a defensiveness that made him keep me at arm's length his whole life.

Yet when I look into the face of my Father as he is described in Scripture, I see a completely different image. When I approach my Father in heaven, his is the first voice shouting my welcome. His is the first set of arms that wrap themselves around my neck. His is the first jubilant yell that cries out, "Let's have a party! Mikey, my son, has come home!"

You don't believe it? Then let me lead you back to a story we touched on briefly way back in chapter 2 of this book. It's commonly known as the parable of the prodigal son, and in it we are given a glimpse into the personality of God, our Father, who is represented by the father of the prodigal son. The Bible records Jesus telling this story in Luke 15:11–32.

You remember it, don't you? A brash, impatient boy insults his father and insists on gaining his inheritance before the old man has even come close to death. The father complies, transferring untold wealth to the son who then heads out on a wild and raucous journey. He burns through his money like a fire in a haystack, wasting his father's hard-earned cash on wine, women, and fast living.

Finally, years later, he finds himself broke and far away from home. He knows he's embarrassed his father, yet all he wants more than anything is simply to be back in Daddy's presence—even if it is only as a servant or hired hand. So he begins the slow, mournful trudge back to his father's front porch, fully expecting to be received with the disgust and harshness that he deserves.

Now let's let the Scripture pick up the tale from here:

> And he [the son] arose and came to his father. But while he was still a long way off, his father saw him and felt compassion, and ran and embraced him and kissed him. And the son

said to him, "Father, I have sinned against heaven and before you. I am no longer worthy to be called your son."

But the father said to his servants, "Bring quickly the best robe and put it on him, and put a ring on his hand and shoes on his feet. And bring the fattened calf and kill it, and let us eat and celebrate. For this my son was dead and is alive again; he was lost and is found."

And they began to celebrate.

verses 20–24 ESV

Do you see what I see in this passage? Do you see the breathless joy that's written all over the father's response to seeing his son? Can you feel the trembly excitement, the sheer happiness that runs through the man on glimpsing his child once again?

This prodigal's father *welcomed* his son with arms wide open, with joy and passion and hugs and kisses and gifts and a feast and more! I can almost hear him speaking the words, "Welcome home, my son! I'm so glad to see you, to be able to spend time with you, to hear of your joys and sorrows, to share in your pain and happiness, to be a part of the life I helped to create! Welcome, welcome, welcome, my son!"

Friend, each day of your life can be a sweet reunion like that with your heavenly Father. He doesn't sit up on his throne with a stern face and scepter raised to punish you on arrival into his courts. He is like the father Jesus described in this parable—a Daddy who can't wait to see you, to spend time with you, to "hang out" with you, sharing the magical and the mundane moments of this life together.

Think about it. God didn't have to become human to save us. He didn't have to endure a virgin birth, to live out a life here on this earth to bring us back to him. But that's just what Jesus did, leaving the limitlessness of the heavenly realm to hang out here on earth, to spend time physically with humans so that we could learn how to spend time spiritually with him through all of life.

My son and I like to do all kinds of fun things together. We've been to Walt Disney World and ridden all the exciting rides. We've spent a day at the football stadium to watch our much-beloved Cleveland Browns play in person. We've laughed together at the antics of the Harlem Globetrotters, danced and sung along with Steven Curtis Chapman in concert, stood in awe in the presence of the animals at the zoo, played miniature golf, bowled strikes and gutter balls, shot hoops, played video games, and much much more. And at the end of every day, no matter how exciting the events, I always say the same thing to him. "Tony, I had a great day. But do you know what I liked best about today?"

Since he's heard me say this hundreds of times over, he grins and says, "Yeah, Dad. I know. What you liked best was just being *with me*."

And every once in a while he adds, "What I liked best was being with you too."

That's the way God views his relationship with you. It doesn't matter what you and he do during the day—whether you spend a mind-numbing day at work or a thrill-seeking day at Universal Studios, whether you eat alone and watch TV or have a romantic evening with a loved one, or whatever! At the end of the day, if you listen closely, you can hear your Father whispering to you, "My child, do you know what I liked best about today? Being *with you*."

And as you close your eyes to drift off to sleep, you can take comfort in knowing another sweet reunion with God awaits you first thing in the morning. Because, unlike your earthly family and friends, he never gets tired of spending time with you. You see, your Father loves you, it's true, but almost as important is this secondary truth: Your Father *likes* you too.

Your Father Is a Joyful Person

I believe it's important for you and me to understand that God is a joyful person. Too frequently we focus on the other aspects of his character—love, power, omniscience, judgment, and so on—and overlook this vital part of the personhood of the One we call Father. Our Christian brothers and sisters are often no help to us in this. As theologian Helmut Thielicke once said, "The glum, sour faces of many Christians . . . give the impression that, instead of coming from the Father's joyful banquet, they have just come from the Sheriff who has auctioned off their sins and now are sorry they can't get them back again."[5]

I believe Pierre Teilhard de Chardin had the more accurate assessment when he said, "Joy is the surest sign of the presence of God."[6] How true that is—and how easily forgotten! If we were to judge by much of Christendom today, we'd be more likely to say:

Political protests are the surest sign of the presence of God.

Church attendance is the surest sign of the presence of God.

Boycotts of entertainment companies are the surest signs of the presence of God.

Long faces and stern lectures are the surest signs of the presence of God.

T-shirts and bumper stickers bearing faith-based slogans are the surest signs of the presence of God.

The list could go on and on—but it would never be true. What is true is that God is a joyful person, and joy *is* the surest sign of the presence of God. Perhaps this is best seen in the person of Jesus Christ. As philosopher and teacher S. D. Gordon has said, "Jesus is God spelling Himself out in language that man can understand."[7] As such, he gives us glimpses of the Father in ways that no other can.

I think it's interesting to note that the first recorded miracle of Christ in the Bible was one performed at a party. The story is found in John 2:1–11, and it's the account of a time when Jesus turned water into wine to provide drink for the guests at a wedding party. What's attention grabbing to me is not that Jesus could do a miracle of liquid transformation. It's that Jesus was at a party, better yet, that he was *invited* to the party, presumably by people who knew him from his youth.

I love the way Max Lucado explores this fascinating aspect of God in his now-classic book *When God Whispers Your Name*. He says:

> When the bride and groom were putting the guest list together, Jesus' name was included. And when Jesus showed up with a half-dozen friends, the invitation wasn't rescinded. Whoever was hosting this party was happy to have Jesus present.
>
> "Be sure and put Jesus' name on the list," he might have said. "He really lightens up a party."
>
> Jesus wasn't invited because he was a celebrity. He wasn't one yet. The invitation wasn't motivated by his miracles. He'd yet to perform any. Why did they invite him?
>
> I suppose they liked him . . .
>
> May I state an opinion that may raise an eyebrow? . . . I think Jesus went to the wedding to have fun. . . . His purpose wasn't to turn the water into wine. That was a favor for his friends.
>
> His purpose wasn't to show his power. The wedding host didn't even know what Jesus did.
>
> His purpose wasn't to preach. There is no record of a sermon.
>
> Really leaves only one reason. Fun. Jesus went to the wedding because he liked the people, he liked the food, and heaven forbid, he may have even wanted to swirl the bride around the dance floor a time or two. (After all, he's planning a big wedding himself. Maybe he wanted the practice?)[8]

Perhaps this picture of Jesus still isn't enough for you. "Mike," you say, "what you're telling me goes against everything I've been taught about God. Are you sure about this one?"

My answer is a resounding yes! My father-in-law (and seminary professor) Dr. Norm Wakefield backs me up on this. Listen to what he has to say on the subject:

> God is a joyful Person. In fact, He's the one who created joy in the first place, and He wants you to experience it.
>
> A survey through the Bible reveals this to be true. In the New International Version text of the Old and New Testaments, the word joy or one of its variants (such as joyful, rejoice, or rejoicing) is used in 373 separate verses. That's more than one "joy verse" for each day of the year.
>
> Scripture also reveals that the Holy Spirit is a source of joy. He filled Jesus with joy (Luke 10:21), He filled the disciples with joy (Acts 13:52), and He has the power to fill you with joy as well (Romans 15:13; Galatians 5:22).[9]

Today, right now, as I write these words, there is a snowstorm raging outside my window. Some say it has the might to become a blizzard, and I don't doubt that this could be true. But moments ago I paused long enough to look out at the beautiful flakes swirling, spinning, silently crashing down in a blinding blanket of whiteness. To my eyes, there were thousands and thousands of indistinguishable flakes fluttering by. To a Vermont teenager in the 1870s, Wilson Bentley, they were messages from the Creator.

One year for his birthday, Bentley received a microscope as a gift. The curious young man soon trained his scope on a snowflake and discovered it had an intricate, beautiful design. He looked at another, and another, and before long he realized something important: Every snowflake was stunningly designed—and every one was different.

The teen couldn't believe that no one had discovered this before, and he set about painstakingly drawing what he saw for others to see. In all, he drew more than 300 pictures, copying snowflakes he had captured in his microscope. It was no surprise, then, that for his seventeenth birthday his family gave him a new present—a camera that could take pictures through a microscope! It took him two years, but Wilson eventually mastered the equipment and was finally able to capture a snowflake on film. In 1924 the world was finally introduced to Wilson's wonder when the American Meteorological Society published 2,500 of his best snow crystal photos in a book. And of the 2,500 crystals, there were still no two alike.[10]

Now, why would an infinite God go to such lengths to endue each individual snowflake with its own unique beauty and design? It's certainly not a practical use of the Creator's time. After all, snow could fall just as easily in identical round pellets as it could in lighter than air, designer snowflakes. Even the beauty of a snowflake is mostly wasted among God's creatures—it wasn't even recognized by the world populace at large until the twentieth century! And, besides, when was the last time you paused to appreciate the sight of a teeny fleck of frozen moisture?

Really, the design of a snowflake serves no practical purpose and is so small as to be of little aesthetic purpose either. So why has it been given this gift of great beauty and grace? I can think of only one reason—*because it gives the Father joy to do so.*

So today, as I watched the muted frenzy going on inches from my face, I could almost feel God smiling with delight at his work of art. I could almost envision him crafting with lightning speed each new, unique, individual snowflake until he had thousands of them gathered up in his great hands, then laughing with joy as he flung them by the gentle bucketful down on my little space.

Yes, our Father is a person of joyful tendencies. The snowflake tells me so. Now each time I see a little white flurry, I am reminded that there is a God—and he is smiling.

Your Father's Joy Can Be Infectious

We are nearing the end of this book, and I find myself wanting to take great care to leave you one last thought that can be of lasting value to you. I know you have endured much sorrow in your life. I know you have faced difficult situations, physical and financial hardships, emotional trials, and spiritual disappointments. I know that you have often managed to rise above these circumstances and that you will continue to do so tomorrow and the next day and the next.

So what is the final advice I can leave with you? Simply this—*enjoy it.*

Remember, you are the child of God, and he is a joyful person. He delights in you, and you can delight in him. His is a joy that can be infectious, that can prick your soul and spread through it from top to bottom, inside and out.

Sure, your life won't be easy. Enjoy it anyway. Yes, you will always carry in you some of the scars of your parents' divorce. Don't let that prevent you from enjoying your life today. In fact your difficult past may be turned into a blessing if it helps you appreciate this moment you are in, if it leads you to the smiling face of your Father in heaven.

Listen to what legendary author and Christian thinker Madeleine L'Engle says about this:

> I don't envy those who have never known any pain, physical or spiritual, because I strongly suspect that the capacity for pain and the capacity for joy are equal.
>
> Only those who have suffered great pain are able to know equally great joy.[11]

Friend, we've experienced the pain part of this equation. Isn't it about time we chose to experience the joy part as well? Isn't it time to open ourselves up to our Creator and let his joy flood our souls, regardless of our circumstances?

Now, some of you out there may be hesitant to do this. Perhaps you feel you deserve to suffer, or maybe you're just in too much of a rut to try to get out again. For you I have an anonymously penned "Prescription for Unhappiness" that James S. Hewett included in a compilation of inspirational quotes. It goes like this:

1. Make little things bother you: don't just let them, make them!
2. Lose your perspective of things, and keep it lost. Don't put first things first.
3. Get yourself a good worry—one about which you can not do anything but worry.
4. Be a perfectionist: condemn yourself and others for not achieving perfection.
5. Be right, always right, perfectly right all the time. Be the only one who is right, and be rigid about your rightness.
6. Don't trust or believe people or accept them at any thing but their worst and weakest. Be suspicious. Impute ulterior motives to them.
7. Always compare yourself unfavorably to others, which is the guarantee of instant misery.
8. Take personally, with a chip on your shoulder, every thing that happens to you that you don't like.
9. Don't give yourself wholeheartedly or enthusiastically to anyone or to anything.
10. Make happiness the aim of your life instead of bracing for life's barbs through a "bitter with the sweet" philosophy.

Use this prescription regularly and you will be guaranteed unhappiness for as long as you do.[12]

For the rest of us sane people, I want to share with you another story I read in Nancy Stafford's excellent book *Beauty by the Book.* In fact I'm going to let her share it with you here:

> Show me who You really are, Lord! I prayed. Give me a way to understand Your grace. I want to know who You really are.
>
> Immediately a picture of a huge field of yellow daisies came to my mind. Then Jesus' head popped up. He was lying on His back in the daisies.
>
> He grinned. "I'm just lying here looking."
>
> Then I saw Him lying on a cloud, then in the hammock, then on my veranda writing on my laptop computer, then working out in an exercise class, then on a horse on the trail.
>
> "I'm everywhere you want to be. I am in all the true pleasures of life. You will find Me there as much as you will find Me in the drudgery."
>
> Then He got up and waved me over to Him, and we played leapfrog across the field! At that moment I grasped the joy and freedom that comes from being a cherished daughter of God.[13]

What a beautiful picture that is! To finally discover that there is an infectious joy to be found in the arms of God, no matter the past, no matter the present, no matter what the future holds. We have a Father in heaven who cherishes us and who will impart to us his joy that is not of this world—and that cannot be tainted by it either.

And so, as we part company and you turn toward the last pages of this book, let me leave you with this quote from an anonymous, but extremely wise, person: "It's never too late to have a happy childhood."

Friend, your first childhood wasn't perfect. Don't let that stop you from having a happy new childhood as a son or daughter of the great and wonderful God, your very own, adoptive heavenly Father!

Amen!

Something to Think About . . .

Use the following questions either by yourself or with a group to process what you've learned in this chapter.

- Is it difficult for you to accept the idea that God enjoys—and *likes*—you? Why or why not?
- Read the following Bible verses: Psalm 30:5; 32:11; 35:9; Philippians 3:1; 4:4; 1 Thessalonians 5:16; Revelation 21:1–5. What do these passages communicate to you about the importance of joy in God's family?
- When you picture Jesus' face, is it most likely smiling, frowning, or something in between? Why do you suppose that is?
- What can you do to begin a new, happy childhood today?

Something to Do

Plan a party to celebrate the joy of being a child of your heavenly Father! Invite friends and family members, and do something you all enjoy (play games, go to a movie, eat at a restaurant, sit around and chat, cook out, whatever).

At the party give everyone (including yourself) a fresh daisy as a reminder that there is a God—and he is smiling.

AFTERWORD

An Appointment with the Father

I'd be remiss if I ended this book any other way than to allow you an opportunity to add one more story to it—your story.

Perhaps, as you read through the pages here, God's Spirit began speaking to you, calling you to him. Perhaps you've never given your life fully to Jesus Christ. Perhaps it's finally time for you to respond, to make your own meeting with your heavenly Father.

The message is simple. All of us—you included—have done wrong. The Bible calls that sin and reports that the penalty of sin is eternal death. That's the bad news.

The good news is that God sent his Son, Jesus Christ, to pay the penalty of sin. Jesus gave his life, suffering and dying by crucifixion, to pay that penalty. And then, to show that he was more powerful than sin and death, Jesus rose from the dead, coming back to life with an offer of life to all who would believe. He offers life to you.

Listen to how the Bible describes this:

For all have sinned; all fall short of God's glorious standard.

Romans 3:23 NLT

The wages of sin is death, but the free gift of God is eternal life through Christ Jesus our Lord.

Romans 6:23 NLT

For if you confess with your mouth that Jesus is Lord and believe in your heart that God raised him from the dead, you will be saved. For it is by believing in your heart that you are made right with God, and it is by confessing with your mouth that you are saved. As the Scriptures tell us, "Anyone who believes in him will not be disappointed."

Romans 10:9–11 NLT

And so now we are back to you. Would you like to experience the forgiveness and renewed life that God, your Father, offers you? If so, it's only a prayer away.

Open your heart to Jesus right now. Pray to him. Ask him to forgive the failings of your past, to erase the penalty of your sin. Ask him to fill you with his Holy Spirit, to enable you to follow him for the rest of your life, to formally adopt you into the family of God.

Why not do it now?

After you have prayed, please contact a church near you and let someone know about it. Tell the folks there that you have just given your life to Jesus and would like help to learn more about following him.

And if you think of it, drop me an e-mail to let me know about your new story too. I'd love to hear from you. You can e-mail me through the "contact us" page on my web site, www.Nappaland.com.

I look forward to hearing from you soon.

NOTES

Introduction Just the Facts

1. Furstenberg et al., "Life Course," 656, quoted in Maggie Gallagher, *The Abolition of Marriage* (Washington, D.C.: Regnery Publishing, 1996), 76.

2. "Divorce Rates Plunge in 25 Community Marriage Policy Cities," http://www.marriagesavers.com/divorcerates.htm.

3. Barna Research Group, "Christians Are More Likely to Experience Divorce than Are Non-Christians," press release (21 December 1999), http://www.barna.org/cgi-bin/MainTrends.asp.

4. Barna Research Group (21 December 1999), http://www.barna .org/cgi-bin/MainTrends.asp.

5. David Blankenhorn, "Fatherhood Uprooted," *Touchstone Magazine* (2001). See http://www.touchstonemag.com/docs/issues/14.1docs/14-1pg20.html.

6. Ibid.

7. "The Price of Dividing," http://www.maritalstatus.com/divorce/articles/dividing.html.

8. Barna Research Group (21 December 1999), www.barna.org/cgi-bin/MainTrends.asp.

9. Arlene Saluter, "Marital Status and Living Arrangements: March 1994," series P20-484 (Washington, D.C.: U.S. Bureau of the Census, March 1996), vi.

10. John W. Whitehead, *Grasping for the Wind* (Grand Rapids: Zondervan, 2001), 255.

11. Barna Research Group (21 December 1999), http://www.barna .org/cgi-bin/MainTrends.asp.

12. Brian Willats, "Breaking Up Is Easy to Do," citing statistical abstract of the United States (Michigan Family Forum, 1993).

13. Ibid.

14. Ibid.

15. Gallagher, *The Abolition of Marriage*, 76.

16. Andrew J. Cherlin, *Marriage, Divorce, Remarriage* (Cambridge: Harvard University Press, 1981), 71, quoted in Gallagher, *The Abolition of Marriage*, 77.

17. Willats, "Breaking Up Is Easy to Do," citing statistics from National Center for Health Statistics, U.S. Department of Health and Human Services.

18. Gallagher, *The Abolition of Marriage*, 117; Dennis A. Ahlburg and Carol J. DeVita, "New Realities of the American Family," Population Bulletin 47, no. 2 (August 1992): 15.

19. Wade Horn and Andrew Bush, "Fathers, Marriage, and Welfare Reform," Hudson Institute Executive Briefing, 1997, Hudson Institute, Herman Kahn Center, 5395 Emerson Way, Indianapolis, IN 46226, (317) 545-1000. Quoted and condensed from National Center for Policy Analysis, "Making Ideas Change the World," *Policy Digest* (28 July 1997).

20. Census Bureau, http://www.census.gov/population/www/socdemo/ hh-fam.html.

21. Peter Hill, "Recent Advances in Selected Aspects of Adolescent Development," *Journal of Child Psychology and Psychiatry* 34, no. 1 (1993): 69–99, quoted in Gallagher, *The Abolition of Marriage*, 72.

22. Robert E. Emery, *Marriage, Divorce, and Children's Adjustment* (Newbury Park, Calif.: Sage Publications, 1988), 57, 67, quoted in Gallagher, *The Abolition of Marriage*, 60.

23. Deborah A. Dawson, "Family Structure and Children's Health and Well-Being: Data from the National Health Interview Survey on Child Health," *Journal of Marriage and the Family* 53 (1991): 573–79.

24. *Los Angeles Times,* 16 September 1985, cited in Daniel Amneus, *The Garbage Generation* (London: Primrose Press, 1990).

25. *The Legal Beagle*, July 1984, cited in Amneus, *The Garbage Generation*, 113.

26. Judith Wallerstein, "The Long-Term Effects of Divorce on Children: A Review," *Journal of the American Academy of Child and Adolescent Psychiatry* (May 1991): 352.

27. Dorothy Tysse and Margaret Crosbie-Burnett, "Moral Dilemmas of Early Adolescents of Divorced and Intact Families: A Qualitative and

Quantitative Analysis," *Journal of Early Adolescence* 13, no. 2 (May 1993): 168–82.

28. Emery, *Marriage, Divorce, and Children's Adjustment,* 50–54, cited in Gallagher, *The Abolition of Marriage,* 35.

29. Eberstadt, "Infant Mortality," 38, cited in Gallagher, *The Abolilion of Marriage,* 95.

30. Dawson, "Family Structure and Children's Health," 573–79.

31. Carmen Noevi Velez and Patricia Cohen, "Suicidal Behavior and Ideation in a Community Sample of Children: Maternal and Youth Reports," *Journal of the American Academy of Child and Adolescent Psychiatry* 273 (1988): 349–56.

32. Lee Robins and Darrel Regier, *Psychiatric Disorders in America: The Epidemiologic Catchment Area Study* (New York: Free Press, 1991), 103.

33. Sara McLanahan and Gary Sandefur, *Growing Up with a Single Parent: What Hurts, What Helps* (Cambridge: Harvard University Press, 1994), 41.

34. Ibid., 53.

35. Horn and Bush, "Fathers, Marriage, and Welfare Reform."

Chapter 1 A Father Who Is There for You

1. John Trent, *Choosing to Live the Blessing* (Colorado Springs: WaterBrook Press, 1998), 14–23.

Chapter 2 A Father Who Loves You

1. This account adapted and reprinted from Mike Nappa and Norm Wakefield, *Legacy of Joy* (Ulrichsville, Ohio: Promise Press, an imprint of Barbour Publishing, 1998), used by permission.

2. Margaret Wise Brown, *The Runaway Bunny* (1942; reprint, New York: HarperCollins, 1970).

3. *Pee-Wee's Big Adventure,* DVD, Warner Bros., 1985, 2000.

4. Judith S. Wallerstein, Julia M. Lewis, and Sandra Blakeslee, *The Unexpected Legacy of Divorce* (New York: Hyperion, 2000), xix.

5. Ibid., xvi.

Chapter 3 A Father Who Understands You

1. Ambrose Bierce, *The Devil's Dictionary* (1911; reprint, New York: Dover Publications, 1993), 131.

2. "Oddest Warning Labels Recognized," *Reporter-Herald* (Loveland, Tex.), 24 January 2002, A-6.

3. Name changed to protect privacy.

4. A. W. Tozer, *The Knowledge of the Holy* (San Francisco: Harper & Row, 1961), 60.

5. Wallerstein, Lewis, and Blakeslee, *The Unexpected Legacy of Divorce,* 298.

6. Wil is my grandfather-in-law.

7. Neil T. Anderson and Dave Park, *Stomping Out Depression* (Ventura, Calif.: Regal, 2001), 132–33; italics mine.

Chapter 4 A Father Who Accepts You

1. Edward K. Rowell, ed., *Fresh Illustrations for Preaching & Teaching* (Grand Rapids: Baker, 1997), 8.

2. Dr. Peter Hirsch, *Success by Design* (Minneapolis: Bethany, 2002), 50–51.

3. Mike Smith, *Reporter-Herald* (Loveland, Tex.), 26 May 2001, A-4.

4. "Wedding between Strangers Criticized," *Reporter-Herald* (Loveland, Tex.), 26 January 1999, A-10.

5. Quoted in Charles R. Swindoll, *The Tale of the Tardy Oxcart* (Nashville: Word, 1998), 3.

6. Ibid.

7. Neil T. Anderson, *Who I Am in Christ* (1993; reprint, Ventura, Calif.: Regal, 2001), 77.

8. Ibid., 78.

9. Ron Mehl, *The Cure for a Troubled Heart* (Sisters, Ore.: Multnomah, 1996), 67–68.

10. You can read the original story of the "woman at the well" in John 4:4–42 in the Bible.

11. Linda Carlson Johnson, *Mother Teresa: Protector of the Sick* (Woodbridge, Conn.: Blackbirch Press, 1991), 6–10.

Chapter 5 A Father Who Disciplines You

1. Quoted in *Bible Illustrator 3,* CD-ROM, Parsons Technology, 1990–1998.

2. Josh McDowell, *The Father Connection* (Nashville: Broadman & Holman, 1996), 129–32.

3. John C. Maxwell, *The Right to Lead* (Nashville: J. Countryman, 2001), 13–14.

4. Harold L. Willmington, *Willmington's Bible Handbook* (Wheaton: Tyndale House, 1997), 760.

5. McDowell, *The Father Connection,* 127–28.

6. Jim Bakker with Ken Abraham, *I Was Wrong* (Nashville: Thomas Nelson, 1996).

7. Ray Pritchard, *FAQ* (Nashville: Broadman & Holman, 2001), 111.

8. *God's Little Devotional Book for Leaders* (1997; reprint, Tulsa: Honor Books, 2001), 176.

9. "Why We Love Children," *Tidbits* 7, no. 6 (6 February, 2002): 1.

10. Hirsch, *Success by Design,* 72.

11. Don Campbell, Wendell Johnston, John Walvoord, and John Witmer, *The Theological Wordbook* (Nashville: Word, 2000), 95–96.

12. Quoted in *Bible Illustrator 3.*

13. *Hoosiers,* DVD, Orion Pictures, 1986, 2000.

14. Quoted in George Hetzel Jr., *The Coaches' Little Playbook* (Nashville: Cumberland House, 1996), 46.

Chapter 6 A Father Who Forgives You

1. See Barbara Olson, *The Final Days* (Washington, D.C.: Regnery Publishing, 2001), 124–41.

2. George Thomas Kurian, ed., *Nelson's New Christian Dictionary* (Nashville: Thomas Nelson, 2001), 338.

3. Millard J. Erickson, *The Concise Dictionary of Christian Theology,* rev. ed. (Wheaton: Crossway, 2001), 70.

4. Lawrence O. Richards, *Expository Dictionary of Bible Words* (Grand Rapids: Zondervan, 1985), 289.

5. Richard A. Steele Jr. and Evelyn Stoner, *Heartwarming Bible Illustrations* (Chattanooga: AMG Publishers, 1998), 149.

6. H. Norman Wright, *Always Daddy's Girl* (1989; reprint, Ventura, Calif.: Regal, 2001), 237–38.

7. See Mike Nappa and Paul Neale Lessard, eds., *Super Plays for Worship and Special Occasions* (Loveland, Colo.: Group Publishing, 1994), 72–81.

8. Anderson, *Who I Am in Christ,* 110–11.

9. From a September 1998 Nappaland Communications Inc. interview with Max Lucado.

10. Quoted in M. Scott Peck, ed., *Abounding Grace* (Kansas City, Mo.: Ariel Books/Andrews McMeel Publishing, 2001), 40.

11. Ibid., 38.

12. Nancy Stafford, *Beauty by the Book* (Sisters, Ore.: Multnomah, 2002), 52–53.

13. Quoted in Peck, ed., *Abounding Grace*, 38.

14. Marilyn Elias, "To Err Is Human," *Reader's Digest* (January 2002): 188.

15. Mitch Albom, *Tuesdays with Morrie* (New York: Doubleday, 1997), 164–67.

16. James Emery White, *Life-Defining Moments* (Colorado Springs: WaterBrook Press, 2001), 120.

17. R. Kent Hughes, ed., *1001 Great Stories and Quotes* (Wheaton: Tyndale House, 1998), 170–71.

18. Max Lucado, *God Came Near* (Sisters, Ore.: Multnomah, 1986), 89, 92.

Chapter 7 A Father Who Comforts You

1. Wayne A. Detzler, *New Testament Words in Today's Language* (Wheaton: Victor, 1986), 84.

2. From an April 1998 Nappaland Communications Inc. interview with The Martins.

3. George MacDonald, *3000 Quotations from the Writings of George MacDonald*, comp. Harry Verploegh (Grand Rapids: Revell, 1996), 58.

4. Adapted and reprinted from "The LOL and the Boxer" by Dr. Norm Wakefield. Copyright © 1999 by Norm Wakefield. All rights reserved. Reprinted by permission.

5. From a May 1997 Nappaland Communications Inc. interview with John Cox.

6. From a June 1999 Nappaland Communications Inc. interview with Philip Yancey.

7. From a July 1997 Nappaland Communications Inc. interview with Jars of Clay.

8. Ron Mehl et al., *Finding God's Peace in Perilous Times* (Wheaton: Tyndale House, 2001), 140–41.

0. Mike Nappa, Amy Nappa, and Beth Rowland, *KidsOwn Worship Video: FaithWeaver Children's Church, Fall 2001* (Loveland, Colo.: Group Publishing, 2001).

Chapter 8 A Father Who Challenges You

1. You can read about this event in Mark 6:30–44 in the Bible.

2. Rick Reilly, "In Like Flynn," *Sports Illustrated* (11 February 2002): 108.

3. Ibid.

4. William J. Bennett, ed., *The Moral Compass* (New York: Simon & Schuster, 1995), 325.

5. This story is related in *The Moral Compass*, 325–27.

6. Erickson, *The Concise Dictionary of Christian Theology*, 46.

7. Richards, *Expository Dictionary of Bible Words*, 208.

8. Marnie Winston-Macauley, *A Little Joy, A Little Oy: Jewish Wit and Wisdom* (Kansas City, Mo.: Andrews McMeel Publishers, 2001), 188–89.

9. Wallerstein et al., *The Unexpected Legacy of Divorce*, 62.

10. Ibid., 62–63.

11. Stafford, *Beauty by the Book*, 70.

12. White, *Life-Defining Moments*, 51–52.

13. Wallerstein et al., *The Unexpected Legacy of Divorce*, 63; italics mine.

14. Hirsch, *Success by Design*, 24.

15. Lucado, *God Came Near*, 97–100.

16. Steven Curtis Chapman, *Declaration*, CD, Nashville, Sparrow Records, 2001.

17. Steven Curtis Chapman, *Declaration Song by Song*, press materials, 2001.

Chapter 9 A Father Who Empowers You

1. Dave and Neta Jackson, *Hero Tales*, vol. 2 (Minneapolis: Bethany, 1997), 81–85.

2. This story is related in Hirsch, *Success by Design*, 42.

3. This story is related in Bennett, ed., *The Moral Compass*, 309–11.

4. Quoted in Edythe Draper, *Draper's Book of Quotations for the Christian World* (Wheaton: Tyndale House, 1992), entry 5777.

5. Quoted in *Bible Illustrator 3*.

6. Draper, *Draper's Book of Quotations for the Christian World*, entry 5778.

7. From an August 1998 Nappaland Communications Inc. interview with Nikki Leonti.

8. This story is related in Christopher L. Coppernoll, *Soul2Soul* (Nashville: Word, 1998), 178–81.

9. *Bible Illustrator 3*.

10. Billy Graham, *Day by Day 2002 Calendar* (Wheaton: Tyndale House, 2001), February 15 entry.

11. Don Campbell et al., *The Theological Wordbook*, 147–48.

12. Philip Yancey, *What's So Amazing about Grace?* (Grand Rapids: Zondervan, 1997), 13.

13. Ibid., 14.

14. W. H. Lewis, ed., *Letters of C. S. Lewis* (New York: Harcourt Brace Jovanovich, 1966), 250.

15. Steele and Stoner, *Heartwarming Bible Illustrations,* 194–95.

16. Graham, *Day by Day 2002 Calendar,* March 4 entry.

17. Quoted in Peck, *Abounding Grace,* 196.

Chapter 10 A Father Who Enjoys You

1. Ross and Kathryn Petras, *The 176 Stupidest Things Ever Done* (New York: Main Street Books/Doubleday, 1996), 12.

2. Ibid., 84.

3. *Nelson's Complete Electronic Library of Stories, Sermons, Outlines, and Quotes,* CD-ROM (Nashville: Thomas Nelson, 2000).

4. Winston-Macauley, *A Little Joy, A Little Oy,* 97–98.

5. Quoted in *Bible Illustrator 3.*

6. Quoted in Swindoll, *The Tale of the Tardy Oxcart,* 322.

7. Quoted in *The Book of Wisdom* (Sisters, Ore.: Multnomah, 1997), 454.

8. Max Lucado, *When God Whispers Your Name* (Nashville: Word, 1994), 22–25.

9. Mike Nappa and Norm Wakefield, *The Heart of a Father* (Ulrichsville, Ohio: Barbour, 1998), 156–57.

10. "Snowflake Bentley," *Focus on the Family Clubhouse* (March 2002): 12.

11. Quoted in *Bible Illustrator 3.*

12. James S. Hewett, *Illustrations Unlimited* (Wheaton: Tyndale House, 1988), 281.

13. Stafford, *Beauty by the Book,* 110–11.

Mike Nappa is an award-winning and best-selling author of many books, including, *Who Moved My Church?*, *The Courage to Be Christian*, *Tuesdays with Matthew,* and *A Heart Like His.* He has also published hundreds of articles and served as a columnist for several prominent publications like *Focus on the Family* (Growing Years Edition), *HomeLife, FaithWorks, Christian Single, ParentLife, Living with Teenagers, CBN.com, Crosswalk.com,* and more.

Additionally, Mike is the founding publisher of the award-winning web site Nappaland.com, *"The Free Webzine for Families,"* and creator of *Focus on the Family Clubhouse's* award-winning children's comic *Johnny Grav & The Visioneer.*

A former youth pastor, Mike studied theology and Christian education at Biola University. He now makes his home in Colorado where he is active in his church.

To contact Mike, access his free webzine for families at www.Nappaland.com.